FIVE-STAR REVIEWS FROM READERS

"I just finished the entire book. For me, it was one of those, 'I cannot put this down until I finish it!!!!' Kimberly is an excellent writer and kept my interest throughout the whole book, as I could connect with almost everything she shared. From the lack of commitment to myself [to] searching for the right one and not giving in to just any relationship, [this book] remind[ed] me how to love myself [and that] the greatest lessons are gained from being the teacher, accepting help, living in joy and awakening into my Divine Self. Wow, wow, wow . . . READ THIS BOOK!!!!"

— Kathleen Rogers-Vanleeuwen

• • •

"[If you have] had unexplainable experiences of Oneness, unexpected and powerful connections, [or] questions about [your] reason for being here, this book is for you. Kim generously shares her journey from a place of grace and authenticity with the intention of opening her readers up to the Truth of their Being. This is a book about Love in its purest and truest sense."

— Franne Demetrician

"As a Metaphysical Minister and an avid reader, I was excited to discover this book and learn more about twin flames. Right from the beginning I realized this book was something more powerful than an explanation of what a twin flame is and the author's view of it.

"Kimberly is an excellent writer, and her story is very open, candid, and honest. She immediately captivated me, and I began to realize that while the book is about twin flames, it is also a powerful story of love. Not in the kind we generally think of that's portrayed in the movies but something so much, much more. I won't spoil it for you and assure you that you will fall in love with the author as well as deeper in love with yourself after reading this book."

— Michelle Spalding

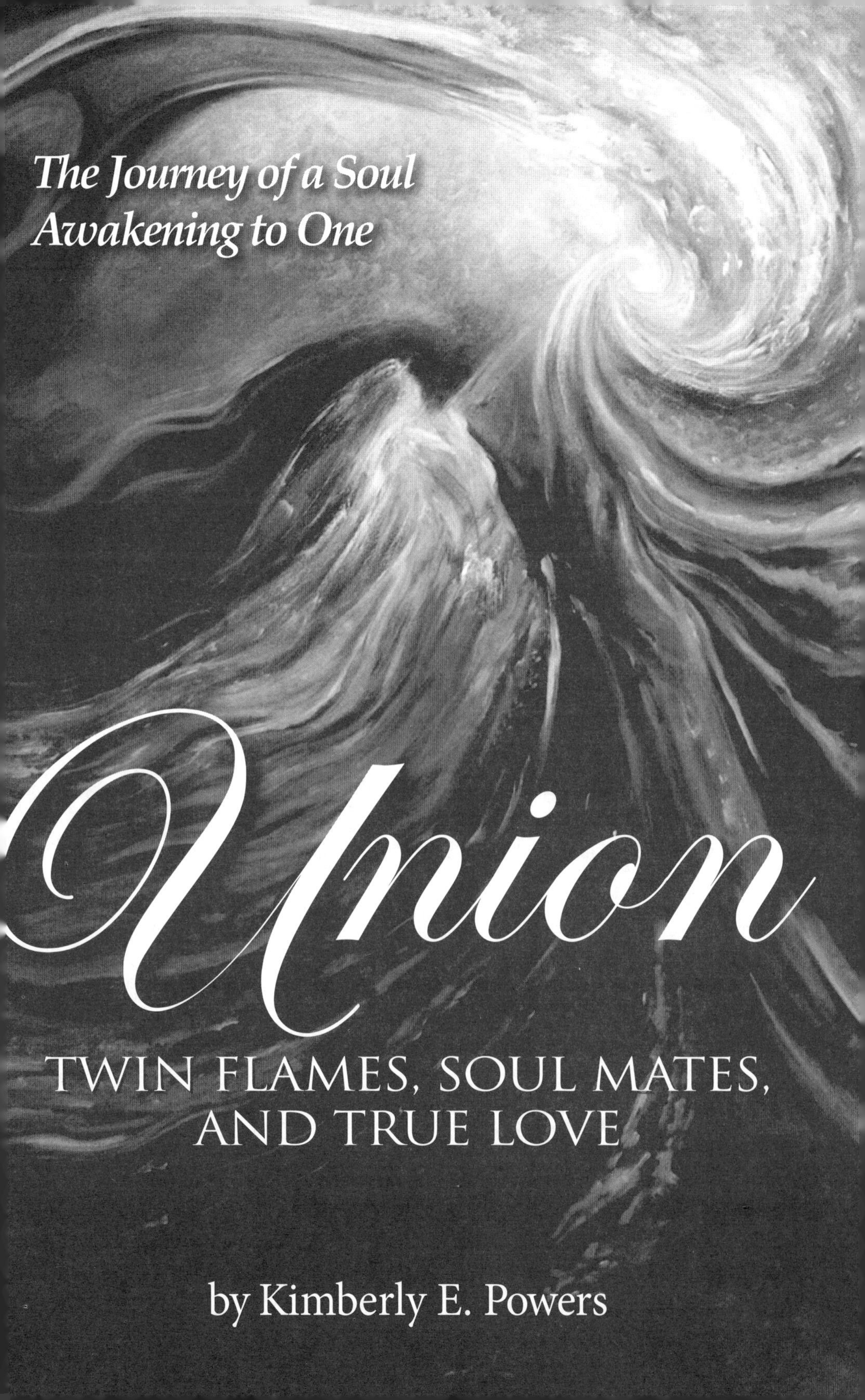

The Journey of a Soul Awakening to One

Union

TWIN FLAMES, SOUL MATES, AND TRUE LOVE

by Kimberly E. Powers

Union

TWIN FLAMES, SOUL MATES, AND TRUE LOVE

The Journey of a Soul Awakening to One

by Kimberly E. Powers

LIGHT Technology PUBLISHING

For more information about special discounts for bulk purchases, please contact Light Technology Publishing Special Sales at 1-800-450-0985 or publishing@LightTechnology.net.

Cover art by Rassouli
Feather art by Caresse VanPelt

ISBN-13: 978-1-62233-019-5
Published and printed in the United States of America by:

Light Technology Publishing

PO Box 3540
Flagstaff, AZ 86003
800-450-0985
www.LightTechnology.com

DEDICATION

This book is dedicated to the men in my life.

To my sons: Quentin, because you know my soul so deeply and completely and hold me to my truth. Nathan, for your unconditional love and for teaching me how important I am to you and the world. It has been my greatest joy to be the mom to two of the most remarkable young men I have ever met.

To my dad, because your unending love and support gives me strength beyond words.

And lastly, to my grandfather, who is always with me showing me how much I am loved.

TABLE OF CONTENTS

A NOTE FROM THE AUTHOR

I wrote this book because I have asked questions and found answers that I believe will help you understand the nature of relationships and why we create them. I want you to know you are not alone and you are loved beyond your imagination. You are divinity in physical form, and you are here to learn to *live in love*.

I invite you to write to me and ask questions and share your stories with me. I read everything, and I hope every word you read will resonate with you, comfort you, and assure you that all is well and exactly as it should be. This book is a spiritual novel, and I have shared the raw truths of what I have learned on my journey. I have changed names and a few places to honor and respect those who shared my journey.

It is with deep gratitude that I share the story of finding my Twin Flame with you. Through the pages, it is my desire that you learn to live in love with who you are and with everything you have, and together — one by one — we will learn to live in love as one.

— Kimberly E. Powers

PREFACE

We are born with divine grace, each perfect in our connection with God and All That Is. With each breath, we become more human and less godlike until the time comes when we can no longer suppress the aching awareness that there is something more. That's when the remembering begins.

There is only one existence. All things are one, all consciousness is one, and all forms are one. By our own choice, we lose this understanding when we enter this physical world. We come forth in form to find an understanding of expansion through experience. We are God. There is no truth in the concept that we are separate from God or from any other form of existence. The only truth of our separateness is in the way we choose to experience God/ourselves. Often, we hear mystics and metaphysicians refer to our experience as an illusion or even "the Matrix." What some may call an illusion, I believe we can simply call reality if we redefine the word "reality" to mean "what seems to be" rather than "what is the only truth." God is the energy of creation itself, and we each create our own realities.

However, in our physical bodies, we are one being with one energy that gives us life, but we have not realized this. When we choose to leave these bodies and this reality, allowing our energy to dissolve back into the ease of All That Is, our physical selves also dissolve into the earth's energy, and we believe we no longer exist. Yet for millennia, death was how we were able to remember our connection to God and who we are.

At this moment, a shift in our experience has happened. Our bodies are changing, our remembrances are flooding us, and we are beginning to allow our essence — our energy — to move with this physical energy. Now we are beginning to exist much like God does: as a divine being of one.

This organization of our bodies can assist us in understanding our relationship with All That Is (the energy that is God), because we organize and form in much the same way. Our physical bodies are organized into individual cells that are energy transmitters. The cells are still one with the body and ultimately with God but are also separate functioning pieces of the One, each cell organized to experience something different and serve the bigger structure seamlessly.

We recognize the parts of the body individually, such as a hand, a leg, a heart, a tooth, and the like, but it is still one body. I know at moments we feel as though our bodies are not always in sync with themselves and our thoughts. For instance, those moments when my foot falls asleep make me think about how our existence has functioned for so long. Everyone is not always on the same page, even though that is the ultimate design. I have chosen to write this book for those of us who are on the leading edge of our remembrance. It is for those of us who are looking for answers — searching through books, browsing the Internet, and talking to each other in an attempt to understand the pieces we are beginning to remember about relationships to each other and the whole.

The focus of this book is our twin flame relationships. Although when I began writing this book I meant it to be a slow, simple way to catch everyone up to speed on the basics of remembrance, I have since been redirected to speak to those who do not need an explanation of how we are all connected, how we each create our realities, and how the laws of the universe work in our daily lives. So I share with you what I have come to know through my readiness and desire to find my twin flame and ultimately recognize my divine goddess self and my purpose.

I found my twin flame, which I share with you in chapter 6. However, since that experience, I have discovered many more questions, and I have spent much time in deep meditation searching for the answers. I have discovered answers for those who are like me — those asking, reading, and searching for the same answers — and for those who will soon meet their beloved twin flames. My focus has been reduced to that of twin relationships and what is left beyond the union.

Early on, I learned that my own discernment was always what I needed to trust. The information and answers I have found from others have only partially resonated with me. Usually pieces were there, but I have continually felt that something was missing, something different that was yet to be told. So as with anything in life, let your own discernment be your guide.

My story spans twenty-two years, but my focus is on the last three years of my journey. I will teach you how I called in the One and how the One I called forth was God — and me.

Throughout my story, I use "God," "All There Is," "the Universe," and "the Collective Consciousness" as interchangeable names for the same being. The truth is, I do not like to name a higher power in just one way, because to name it is to contain it. I don't believe you can ever name such a divine force, because each moment we take a breath, it is ever-expanding and ever-changing, and we are part of that expansion. Through our willingness to open our hearts, we become more connected to that which we are also creating.

Before I begin my story, I want to take this moment to thank you for becoming a part of my journey and for allowing me to become a part of yours.

ACKNOWLEDGMENTS

On a long journey, there are many who show up to help you achieve your quest. Some are mentors giving you strength, some are adversaries showing you lessons yet to be learned, some are jokesters to keep things light, and some are messengers only to enter for a brief moment. Every one of them is important, no matter how powerful, brief, or painful the assistance was. I open my heart with my deepest gratitude of each who came into my life during my experience of living the journey and writing the book, ultimately publishing it.

My gratitude extends to the readers of *Union*. You are also part of my journey. And now I am part of yours. I hope I am a pleasant part; that is my intention.

To Elizabeth Gilbert, although I have never met you, you have been the catalyst for much of this journey. I'm sorry I cursed you so many times before. You and your messages continue to inspire me to show up and do my part.

Thanks to Mike Dooley for the gift of Infinite Possibilities — the Art of Changing Your Life — and all the Ippies. Their boundless love for each other and unabated faith that dreams do come true are priceless. Your messages, kindness, and support awed me and picked me up time and time again.

To April Joy Rain, my content editor, without your dedication to making dreams into reality, this book would not exist. To Jennifer Sutton, my writing editor, thank you for so generously supporting me and allowing me to give my voice to the world.

To Tinker, who proves how connected we all are, thank you and the team at Light Technology Publishing. I am happy to know our journey together has only just begun.

INTRODUCTION

Soul mates are a part of our everyday lives. I see dating websites filled with bios of people who are searching for their soul mates. I love knowing that we desire deep connections; soul mates can provide us with those connections. What most people on these websites do not understand is that we have many soul mates. Some are seeking the one — the twin flame. They can feel that person exists somewhere, and they are asking, even yearning in some cases, for that deep connection that we feel within our own souls. This calling forth is one of the many reasons so many twins are coming together now. It is we who are bringing this twin energy to Earth at this time. It is we who are shifting the planet into divine love from darkness, and as we are doing this, the universe is answering us through the law of attraction. It must.

People who are looking for their twin flames, whether they know that term or not, are looking for the kind of relationship that brings union — a merging from two into one. They seek moments filled with peace and joy when doing nothing other than simply being together side by side.

However, the one they seek is not actually "the one" person who will bring them joy and happiness but rather the feeling of oneness — union with all things. This is what a twin flame relationship will bring forth. Many who study twin flames refer to this coming together right now as a means to usher in the Christ consciousness on our planet. A term that years ago I heard only once in passing in a metaphysical bookstore has now become the new age of love. Just a little over a year ago when I mentioned I was writing a book about meeting my twin flame, many questioned what that was. Now, only a few years later, people are seeking me out to assist them in understanding these relationships.

Due to the cosmic energy now flooding the earth, we are all searching for our purpose and meaning for being here, and the twin flame is a gateway to discovering who we truly are. I see this very much like the chicken-and-egg scenario. Which came first, the desire to have a life of purpose or to live in love? The answer is obvious to me: As we are one with God and the universe, it is simultaneous; one doesn't come before the other. We are part of the all-knowing and all-remembering and thus working hand in hand, side by side. Our purpose and love are the same thing. Others who study or write about twin flames speculate whether the twin relationship is just an advanced soul mate. I do not find this to be completely the case.

Soul mates are relationships that have agreements to teach and remind us. The relationships allow us to experience each other in different ways. Soul mates come in many forms, such as friends, lovers, parents, children, siblings, and even enemies. These wonderful relationships bring with them a divine recognition — a remembrance of another person. Each of these relationships focuses on exterior issues. The work that is done within them has been said to be karmic. Clearing, balancing, and healing are all forms and functions of soul mate relationships. They are necessary parts of a twin flame journey.

You can recognize soul mate relationships by your emotions: They intensify your emotions. For example, you can feel you love someone so much that you could burst at the seams; or you can hate someone so much that you feel you could physically harm them. There is an intensity of attraction with soul mates unlike in other relationships.

Soul family relationships are those with next-door neighbors you have known for years or with someone you might marry because you dated and eventually fell in love and it was the next thing to do together. However, soul mates know you on an intimate level. They have a way to reach into your heart and connect with you — and you to them. You have shared past lives together, and you will find that there is synchronicity in how you come together.

These relationships are magical and wonderful, and everyone in the world should be lucky enough to experience this union at some point in their lives. They can also prove to be difficult relationships because they teach us karmic life lessons, and this learning can be challenging at times, especially if we do not have the perspective or understanding of the particular life lesson we are learning.

I have had many soul mate relationships. They have been wonderful, and they have been dramatic. Soul mate relationships can last a lifetime. Often those of us who are on the path of spiritual enlightenment will move through these relationships rather quickly. If you happen to stay in one because of any of countless reasons, you can live a happy life. However, for those of us seeking the reflection of our souls — the One — the misery we can endure as a result of staying in a soul mate relationship is beyond painful.

In some cases, we are left with no choice other than to create a disaster in our lives that will ultimately force us to leave the situation altogether. This was the case in my marriage. Rather than leave when I was unhappy, I stayed. I felt duty-bound as a Catholic and a mother. For those looking in, it appeared that I had all the elements of a really wonderful life. However, I was actually desperate and lonely. I felt unworthy of being loved, and as a result of those feelings, I sought exterior success to bring me the feelings I was searching for. I achieved that success, but deep happiness continually eluded me, and eventually the relationship had to end. I created a physical reality of abuse, which was merely an outward manifestation of the interior abuse I was allowing myself to experience.

Now, after doing much interior work on myself, I clearly see that my husband and I had a purpose. Our purpose was to create our children together, and that was it. In retrospect, I remained too long after our purpose was fulfilled, which created more karma for me to heal.

Other soul mate relationships will last a lifetime. My best friend from college, my chemistry teacher from high school, and many others have shown up in my life after years of us not speaking to each other. Their love for me, and my love for them, removes every second that we have been apart. Each of these relationships teaches me something valuable every time I interact within them.

Recently, I reconnected on Facebook with my art teacher who was a source of much love in my life. She believed in me enough to encourage me to enroll in art school. My career was based on her unwavering faith in me. Many years later, I posted on Facebook a powerful experience that I had while teaching at a local soup kitchen. I shared the story of a student who permanently altered my life for the better and how in return I changed his. Her response was immediate and validating, as always. She told me that I had always been special and had a natural gift of affecting the lives of the people around me. She said she knew it the first time I walked into her classroom. She told me how happy she was that I finally found my calling in life.

Looking back, I thought I had chosen a career that was my path. I chose to pursue a career in advertising and marketing, which served me well for many years. But there was more to my purpose, and she recognized that. She became my spiritual mother and continues to be. I am sure in another life she was indeed just that.

After my marriage ended, I enjoyed a few serious relationships that were also with soul mates. Each relationship carried a very valuable lesson for me that was an external type of learning. I learned how to find my own voice and be responsible for my happiness in the relationship. I learned how to accept and receive love from others. I learned how to let go when these relationships no longer served me, and more importantly, I learned that I did not want a relationship that focused on something outside of me, something that demanded me to be anything other than the person I truly am. I learned it was time to find myself. Whoever I really was had been long lost while I was busy accommodating those I chose to love in my past.

The journey I am sharing with you will hopefully, in some way, allow you to recognize your own journey to discover your divine self. Whether you have discovered that you are in fact divine, or maybe your heart aches for the One, you will find the reassurance that you are indeed expanding to the whole that you truly exist as. I hope you will find solace in the fact that you are not crazy, unlovable, or doing something wrong. In finding the one, you will find your purpose and how to live in love.

CHAPTER ONE

DISCOMFORT OF THE DISCORD

There exists an echo — an echo of your voice long before you entered this existence. It is your own voice that answers your question, "Is this all there is?" Your deepest wanting, escaping from the confines of your mind, has brought forth a fragment of your connection with God that still exists, and it is answering as you call out in pain and loneliness and confusion.

Standing by the sliding glass doorway, Keith reached out and touched me as he walked past to go inside. My mother and Betty Ann, her best friend and my second mother, sat by the pool. I saw their eyes connect and exchange a silent conversation as they noticed Keith's touch. We had a connection that was undeniable. What that connection was, I wasn't sure.

It was during that week in 1990 that I heard the term "twin soul" for the first time. The only thing I knew was it meant our souls had been born in the same place. Standing there, I wondered if that was true of Keith and me. Were we from the same distant place — some beautiful, starry galaxy where souls were created like the Universe?

When you hear something that resonates so strongly, it's hard to tell whether it is the attention you give to it that makes it come into your reality or whether it is more of a remembering or a recognition of something you are called to understand. I have concluded over the years throughout my spiritual journey that it is both. I am not sure whether I am right; however, I have gathered that since we do have free will as our gift, then as we give our attention to something, we bring it into our reality.

I also believe that we are born into this human form with a divine knowledge and plan. We have a purpose that we decided would be our gift to the Universe and to our own souls. I feel it is by this plan that our instincts are guided. If we listen along the way, we find clues during our physical journeys here on Earth that let us know that yes, we are on the right path.

It is with this sense that I connected to the idea of twin souls. Although the "twin souls" was only a brief mention in a conversation at a small metaphysical bookstore, I knew I wanted to meet the person my soul was "born" with.

Seeing that knowing exchange between my mother and Betty Ann made me wonder whether Keith and me came from the same place. And if we did, would we spend the rest of our lives together?

• • •

Keith eventually proposed to me in December 1993 after years of dating. I was tired of waiting for someone with which to share my future. I had decided to move on with my life, with or without him. As a result, he realized that he was going to lose me if he did not take action. After waiting years for the moment when he realized I was the one for him, the one he wanted to spend his life with, he very unceremoniously asked me to marry him at his kitchen table, sputtering out the words as if they were choking him.

I am aware now that I could have recognized that our souls were not born together. I could have known if only I had stopped to think about it — if only I'd cared. I didn't, however, and even though I knew in my soul that we were from different places in the universe, I knew we were to build a life together. I also knew it would likely be challenging to do so because we were very different people, but I was still willing to walk into creating a life with him.

I picked a day that was perfect for the wedding — October 4, 1994. It was a Sunday. With the help of my best astrologer friends, I had my tarot cards read and our charts done. I knew this was the perfect day for us to unite. And it was. Ten months later, on the morning of our wedding, our friends and family gathered to celebrate with us, smiling as they read our horoscopes in the paper with surprise. The day was perfect for a wedding, as if the angels themselves were smiling on it. Our day was blessed; the horoscope said so.

As I got ready that morning, I knew the marriage was right. It was my path. I was marrying the man I was meant to be with. The doubts disappeared, and the joy of a new life, a new house, and a dream come true filled me with contentment.

The wedding was perfect. I was a beautiful bride, he was a handsome groom, and my beloved priest was marrying us in a stunning church. As we stood together at the altar, each in the glow of our individual candles illuminating our love, we lit the unity candle together as a symbol of two becoming one. It was the moment I'd waited for my entire life, even more so than the words we spoke. It was the unity I searched for throughout my lifetime, but as my soul reached for his, his did not answer. My eyes looked to him, but his eyes were not looking into mine. As the priest happily announced us as the new Mr. and Mrs. Powers to our loved ones, I knew inside that we were not one merged divine soul but two people in love, sharing one name, one house, and one tax return.

The contrast of what my soul desired and what became never left me from that moment forward. A beautiful photo of the candle lighting ceremony at our wedding reminded me every day of the ache that still lived in my soul. I would notice how lovely the photo was, just as our life appeared to be, but the discord I felt between what seemed to be and what actually was only grew as the years passed.

You may be asking what this contrast is that I am talking about. Contrast is a "positive" way for me to say that we did not see eye to eye. Okay, we pretty much did not agree on anything. Contrast is the difference between what you are experiencing and what you wish to experience or, more accurately, what your truth is.

When we were dating and ran into contrast, I wrote it off due to the difference in our ages (there were ten years between us). However, as we moved into marriage and raised a family together, I could see that our own childhood experiences had a huge impact on how we viewed things like marriage and child rearing.

I was raised in a traditional family with the stability of two parents and four grandparents. I had always lived in a beautiful neighborhood where people knew us, and we were involved in the community. I was an only child and participated in everything the family did. My mother was the cookie chairperson for Girl Scouts, and we spent the weekends together working on the family business affairs. We were almost always together. We vacationed in Florida at my grandparents' home. I was the center of the world, and as a child, I was valued as an important member of the family.

Keith did not have a traditional family. He had three brothers and a half-sister. His mother, more or less, took him from his father and moved him and his younger brother around the country with the man she left his father for. After the divorce, she changed Keith's last name and kept him from his father and two older brothers.

He was not allowed to participate in Cub Scouts or various other childhood activities. The focus in his family was simply to serve his mother's needs and desires. The message in his family was that the children were only there to serve, not to be in the way. The adults were what mattered in his family, not the family as a whole. He had never lived in a house that his family owned, so personalizing his room was never allowed. More or less, he never had the ability to express himself or find out who he really was.

Because of his experiences, Keith had very strange views on some things that became intensely frustrating for him as we worked to build a life together. In the early years, I chalked up his strange desire to paint the air vents in our new house colors different from the walls and connect them together with stripes as a way of trying to capture a long-lost opportunity of living in a basement, which all my friends' older brothers had done in the seventies.

The contrast only grew as I began my own advertising agency. Keith's family members were mainly corporate or government employees, whereas mine were self-employed, service-oriented business owners for many generations. The longer we were married, the less we had in common. In fact, other than an address and equal parts of our DNA in our children, we had nothing in common!

In an effort to make our marriage work, or at least keep it livable, I began morphing myself into what he said he wanted me to be. At that time, I was totally clueless about how much more contrast I would create between us. I worked hard at my business and made a successful and profitable company. I paid everything off, including the mortgage and our cars, thinking that maybe financial pressure was the root of our unhappiness.

I tried to be Martha Stewart, the modern-day June Cleaver — the perfect housekeeper, hostess, and chef. I tried to move to a better neighborhood where Keith could relax and spend his days golfing. I even tried sexing it up! I tried everything I could think of, but I was miserable, and so was he. The harder I worked, the more he disliked me. I had thought that the better I was, the more worthy of his love I would be and the happier we would be. Instead, the contrast made him feel more insecure, angry, and less appreciative of all my efforts. He focused solely on tearing me down from the pedestal he believed I was on.

When our marriage finally came tumbling down, in disaster style, I was standing on our balcony and looking down at him in the entryway. Our candle-lighting photo was in the background as he yelled at me: "Do you want a divorce?"

He asked me that question many times in an effort to either get me to behave in the manner he wanted or to create a way for him to leave for a few days while teaching me a lesson. My response had always been to plead with him to stay. I would anoint him with every ounce of love I had. However, this time was different; this time, the fight was not about what I was doing wrong but about our sons wanting a dog. This time, I knew I had to fight for my children to have the lives they wanted and deserved, so this time I said yes. The moment I said it, I felt as though someone had finally removed a heavy cement block off of my shoulders that I hadn't even known was there.

It took me over a year after our divorce was finalized to begin the healing process and start examining what had happened in our marriage. How could it be that the perfect timing and perfect wedding had ended so badly? This is what led me to understand and finally appreciate the relationship for what it was. We were, in fact, soul mates, destined to come together for a reason. And that reason was simply to learn from each other and to create our amazing children.

As I mentioned before, soul mates are *not* twin souls or twin flames, whichever term you prefer. Soul mates come in many types of relationships — friends, family, and yes, even lovers. We feel a recognition with them and a mission to be together. The feelings are intense and instant. Your soul mate may be a person you meet who you feel you have known forever, so you become instant friends. It can be someone you work with and have an intense dislike for, even if you don't know the person at all. Soul mates have shared past lives with us, and before we decided to incarnate into this lifetime together, we agreed to assist each other along the way. These are beautiful relationships, whether they are pleasant to deal with or not. They help us clear our karma, heal our wounds, and work out the world's problems in the microcosm of the soul mate relationship.

Soul mates are from what we call soul families. This simply means that they are from our energy group. As soul mates, we incarnate together over and over again, supporting each other in our souls' expansion and learning.

Keith was definitely my soul mate. We felt a strong familiarity with each other from the beginning of our relationship, but I did not understand the purpose of the relationship at the time. I did not see what he was showing me about myself. Instead, I got lost in the relationship, doing everything possible I could to make it work. I was not yet awake to what I could learn from his reflection.

> "People think a soul mate is your perfect fit, and that's what everyone wants. However, a true soul mate is a mirror, the person who shows you everything that is holding you back, the person who brings you to your own attention so you can change your life."
>
> — Elizabeth Gilbert, *Eat, Pray, Love*

If I had been aware of what a soul mate relationship was, Keith's lack of commitment to me would have shown me that I was not committed to myself, my needs and desires. His lack of care for me could have shown me I was not taking care of myself. Instead, I thought I needed to do more or be different in some way. By changing myself to try to suit his needs, I was getting further and further away from my soul's purpose, which was to live in joy and awaken to my divine self.

It was not until I realized I could no longer live the life I had painted myself into that I began focusing on what I could do to make myself happy. Often, this can be a vicious cycle. We believe that a different person can make us happy. We have a tendency to skip from one relationship, job, or anything else outside of ourselves to the next thing in our pursuit of happiness. Instead, we should focus inward on ourselves. For me, at least, I was beginning to understand it is my responsibility to make my situation what I want it to be. I knew this because I had a successful business that showed me what I positively focused on did indeed work. In other words, I knew it was up to me to create my own reality, and I knew that the one I was living at home was not the reality I wanted or could live any longer.

Although I was no longer in the situation, I was still at a loss as to *how* to create the relationship I so desired. That answer eluded me during my marriage because I never understood exactly what my relationship with Keith was trying to show me about myself. It was not until I went through our divorce that I finally began to believe in myself again. Then I discovered I was actually happier being alone.

It was much easier to be alone and a single parent without support than to have the constant struggle of an unpleasant relationship in the mix. I was finally able to do the things I loved with my sons — traveling, playing, and adopting animals. My gifts and intuitive abilities finally returned. It was then that I began to find my true self. During this time, even though I had a significant amount of financial stress, I tried to trust that all was well because I had lived through the worst situation of my life, and all was finally well with that.

• • •

Soul mate relationships provide us with huge lessons. As we learn from them, we begin to ask new questions and to receive new answers, thus making new discoveries about ourselves. My first question after I realized I was capable and happy being on my own was, "How do you have a good, healthy, happy relationship?" Al Anon, for those of you who may not be familiar with it, is a support group for families of alcoholics. Al Anon was the place I began learning the answer to my question. Keith was an alcoholic, whether he knew it or not, and I knew that people in relationships with alcoholics were more or less likely to repeat the same types of relationships over and over. I was determined to not let that happen to me again.

Because I was focused on healing, my next relationship was about healing. However, I was also focused on *not* finding a relationship that had issues with alcohol. What I missed at the time, but I have since learned, is that the Universe does not hear the word "not" when it comes to our desires. So despite my best effort to avoid a relationship with an alcoholic, I found one.

Although the relationship was very different, alcohol was still an issue. This time, however, the relationship was more positive and healing. I felt the love I was looking for. In fact, the love for me was so strong and gentle that I was able to heal from the abuse and lack of love I had experienced in my marriage. I was learning to see I was valuable and worthy of someone else's love for just being myself. I was beginning to see how the reflection of a loving soul mate relationship worked.

What I didn't see at the time was that I was holding on to fear about my financial security, and my partner was doing the same. That fear began manifesting in our relationship, eventually deteriorating the bond under a negative financial spiral. This time, however, I knew I didn't have to stay and work it out to be worthy of love again. I let go of someone I loved dearly because I had learned to love myself selfishly enough to want my happiness over a partner's presence. This is when I began seeking a higher, more valuable relationship — one with myself.

CHAPTER TWO

ALCHEMY OF THE SOUL

The willing point is a moment in which we consciously accept that we could be within an illusion, that perhaps we don't know everything, or that what we know is not the absolute truth. It is a point where we begin to question what we know to be true and risk allowing ourselves to believe that we have been wrong.

There is a movie that I often watch, and somehow it always gets to me. It's *When Harry Met Sally*. In the movie, two strangers share a happenstance meeting after which their paths continue to cross over a period of many years. Throughout the movie, we see the human masculine-feminine drama play out repeatedly in all its various forms. Like with many movies, I find different meanings each time I watch it. However, some of my favorite parts are the scenes with the little old couples talking about how they met and lived happily ever after.

I always questioned that "happily ever after" concept. I married for that "happily ever after," and I found that, despite my best efforts, it did not exist for me. My subsequent relationships did not provide it either. I was missing something. If I actually found a soul mate, and I knew that we had more than one, then what was finding the One about?

Was the One someone you were supposed to settle with? I understood compromise, but compromise did not seem to be an issue I had. Rather, I felt that each time I was with someone, one of us would have to change virtually everything about ourselves to be with the other in a "forever" relationship. Why was this the case? It did not seem logical that we would plan to come to this amazing planet to experience joy, love, and happiness only to have to give up who we were or watch the one we love be forced to do the same.

I would rather be alone than lose myself again. I wasn't even sure I'd found myself in the first place. Was being alone the ultimate expression of love? I was raised Catholic, and according to tradition, priests and nuns are married to God. I would often sit in church and think how lucky my beloved priest was. He lived in divine union with God and thus was able to devote the majority of his time to God as his center focus.

I loved going to church and listening to my priest. Somehow, despite how little I actually went to church and how crowded it often was, I felt as if he was only speaking to me. Often my sons would notice how he could pick me out in a crowd. This was proven true during a ceremony at my son's Catholic high school, which I attended at the last-minute invitation of my younger son. The ceremony, because of the number of people, was being held in a parking lot. Our priest was among many at this event. He called my name and waved at me. Not realizing when I left the house that I would be attending a ceremony, I was wearing a T-shirt, ripped jeans, and huge sunglasses, so I wasn't sure he was calling to me. But he was. As we hugged each other, I asked him how he could always pick me out in a crowd. His smile always made my heart soft; I felt loved by something beyond him through his eyes. But today he looked at me seriously and said, "You shine, Kimberly. I can't help but see you, no matter where you are."

Just so you know, the dogma of the church makes me crazy — especially the "letter of the law" followers of the faith. But this man, my priest, along with a few others I have had the privilege and honor of knowing throughout the years, is truly what faith is about. This priest connects me to God, and I wanted to feel what it was like, living with this connection day in and day out. So I made it my mission to find out, not based on the traditional Catholic way, but in a way based on the spiritual leaders I have loved throughout the years.

At one time in my life, I ventured into the realm of converting to Judaism. I know this may sound crazy, but I was dating someone who was Jewish. I had many Jewish friends, all of whom I respected very much for their faith. The problem for a non-Jew in dating a Jewish man is that by tradition, the children are born into the faith of the mother. So if I were to marry this man, which was quite possible at the time, I would have to decide whether I could be Jewish or whether I would ask him to convert to Catholicism. I knew it was a rather large gap, one that I ultimately did not bridge, but I really did love learning about the religion. It was be the first of many I studied over the years.

As an art student, I learned that religion and early art go hand in hand. I found the study of faith fascinating, but learning about Judaism struck me in a most unusual way. Jews talked directly to God. I may be stating the obvious when I say that Jews do not recognize Jesus as the Messiah and Lord, but it never occurred to me that I did not pray to God as they do. I often prayed to the saints, I always prayed to Mary and Jesus, but I never realized that I did not have my own direct connection to God. Jesus is awesome, and I often meditate with his presence or that of Mother Mary and even Mary Magdalene, but as Christians, we are taught to pray to Jesus — not God. Through studying Judaism, I learned that I had a direct connection to God and All That Is.

One thing I learned early in my life is that God is not some scary dude who will strike you down if you do something wrong. I learned this lesson when my mother came to church one day to find me locked outside. The church we belonged to did not have the benevolent kind of priests I now know; instead, they had the kind of nuns that scary movies are made of — nuns who taught children that they were wicked and evil and were surely doomed to hell if they did not conform.

This particular day, I was locked outside because my mother did not sign the paper for my confirmation. I was only in third grade, and my only understanding of the concept was that I was allowed to pick a Catholic name. She didn't agree with the change of age from high school to elementary school age the church had recently made. The Church is not fond of people who are not good followers, so the nuns believed that locking me outside, and thereby punishing me, would bring me into alignment with proper Catholic behavior. When my mother arrived to pick me up from the Catholic education class and found me outside, she did the unthinkable. She stormed into the church and, in front of the bloody wooden body of Christ on the cross, unleashed the years of pent-up vengeance for every wrongdoing that any nun had ever inflicted on her and me. And there had been plenty.

I stood terrified in the back of the church, awaiting the impending disaster. I silently sneaked a peek at the ceiling, waiting for the lightning and rolling clouds to send the cathedral down upon our frail bodies. To my amazement, the world did not stop, lightning did not strike, and we left the nun dressed in her habit gasping like a goldfish out of water. It was over. My Catholic education stopped right there. In that moment, I learned the most valuable lesson ever: God doesn't really care about the rules of religion.

• • •

Learning to be alone really changes many aspects of your life. Traditional routines change. There is a certain joy and freedom to that concept, or perhaps it's more of a lack of obligation. I found that in some instances I had less time, and in others I had more. Dinner no longer "had to be at seven" but instead was when I could get it on the table. Rather than dropping off the boys at the soccer field and running home to start dinner while their dad picked them up, I had to stay at practice because there was no time to run back and forth. This made life challenging, but I learned to appreciate the gift of an hour here and there with nothing to do but enjoy watching the boys and appreciate being outside. All the rules in life were being broken, yet the boys and I all seemed to be thriving.

The time I spent on the sidelines of the soccer field is where I began noticing things that others seemed to be missing. Why was I just now noticing images in the clouds? Was my mind making things up to entertain me? I began experimenting with the clouds. I would pose a question to the Universe — to God — and wait. The clouds, which originally existed to me as nothing more than lovely backdrops, would — without fail — move into some shape or form. I wondered if it had meaning or if it was just by my intention that they would change shape.

This lead me to begin researching the subject on the Internet. I busied myself late at night after the boys were asleep, attempting to understand the world around me, a world I never had the time to notice before. I already understood astrology and how the planets affected us through gravitational pulls. I studied many religions, including some ancient indigenous teachings to modern-day movements, but it seemed to me that I was receiving direct communication from a higher power. I wanted to understand more than what I had previously learned, more than what it appeared to be on the surface.

I immersed myself in websites, blogs, and posts sharing information about our ability to communicate and consciously create our desires. I rediscovered Jerry and Esther Hicks, whom I had met years before while they were doing a session on past lives in a local metaphysical bookstore, Planet Earth. Through Esther's connection to the collective called Abraham (usually referred to as Abraham-Hicks), I learned about the law of attraction and the other laws that govern our universe. My mind was open, and I absorbed information like a sponge. Suddenly things began to make sense to me. With the time I would have normally spent watching TV or with my partner, I now had the freedom to explore and discover a new world, one that resonated with me.

I had always believed it wasn't possible that we were the only beings that existed in the universe, and as I learned more, I found others who believed this as well. I found information that connected me to whole communities I did not know existed before. There are many people who have chosen to incarnate on this planet at this time who have similar gifts to mine. Star children, human angels, Indigos, and crystal and rainbow children all have their unique purposes for being here on the planet at this time.

• • •

When I was younger, I tried to hide natural abilities that I discovered were, for me, very normal. As a child, I spoke to angels and Indian spirits who were all around me. I thought everyone did. It was in fourth grade that I discovered this was not the case. During a school assembly, a Native American, who was also my neighbor, pointed me out to the whole school and said "she talks to spirits." Needless to say, my fellow students did not take it well. Apparently, they did not talk to angels nor did they know they could. The harassment was painful, and nothing pleased me more than moving away from that town a year later. When we moved, I decided to leave behind my connection to anything from the beyond. I just wanted to be normal. Now I was remembering and rediscovering the connection that once made me feel different and alone but this time the connection made me feel not so alone.

With my personal life in such an incredible state of evolution, I began feeling restless with my business. What had once given me such joy now seemed meaningless. I felt the calling of something more, something bigger. What, I did not know. And because I didn't have a partner to discuss this with, I spoke to a friend who recommended working with a life coach she knew. I didn't know much about life coaches or their purpose, but I did know that psychologists and the like could not help me. Even worse, if I told them everything I was feeling, learning, and thinking, they would most likely put me away in a padded room!

My work often took me up the coast to Sarasota, so the fact that this "coach" was also in Sarasota served me well in two ways. (1) I really did not want anyone in town to know I was seeing a coach, and (2) it was convenient. During my first meeting with Bri, I spilled out a very edited sense of everything that was going on in my professional life and the dilemmas I was facing. She gave me some very good advice that I had not considered before. I felt very pleased with the session and believed her abilities as a coach were going to be useful. Do we not all dream of having a person to talk to who listens and has great insights into what we are saying without their personal ego getting involved? For a moment, I started to feel satisfied and at ease again. And then something changed. I could see it in her eyes. She saw me, the part of me I meticulously hid away from the world. That fleeting relief of normalcy and ease was once again stolen away, never to be found again. This seemingly normal life coach said to me, "You know there is a bigger picture in all of this, don't you?"

My heart almost stopped. What did she mean by that? Of course I knew. Then the words came out of her mouth, "You are being called forth for a greater purpose, and that is why you are struggling with everything. You are in this world but not of it." The tears instantly flowed from my eyes. Truer words could have never been spoken.

The only thing I could say was, "I don't want to be weird." This response amused her greatly. She was also a soccer mom and understood exactly what I meant. It is hard to be different and feel connected to life when we are more or less seeing through completely different lenses than the rest of the world.

Bri didn't only become my life coach but also my teacher, confidant, and guide through the journey I didn't realize I had already begun. She had the ability to connect to my energy and support me as I navigated the realm I had once left behind. She gave me the confidence that what I was experiencing was true and real. It was her suggestion that led me to begin communicating with the energies beyond that I had stopped listening to so many years before, energies more direct than clouds.

Suddenly, it was as if everything began communicating with me again. I understood the clouds now. Rainbows manifested to delight me, and birds began showing up to guide me. Birds are still big communicators of spirit for me. The Native Americans believe in the presence of animals as spirit guides and teachers. I learned this language before, as a child, and I was again connecting to the universal energies that I once knew so well.

I was able to center myself in the midst of craziness and find my peace, knowing all was well and that I was supported by the abundance of the Universe. I began playing with the energy, and I would delight in manifesting things at whim. I loved setting up a meeting with a client by merely repeating the time I wanted to meet over and over in my mind, only to have them respond asking me to meet at that time. I was thrilled that every place I went I had a parking space waiting for me in the front row. Life was becoming full of joy and ease. But I knew I was missing something. There was an ache deep within my soul, a loneliness, and no matter what delightful things were happening in my life on the surface, there was a wound beneath that never fully healed. If I could only figure out what it was.

CHAPTER THREE

ONE WITH THE MOUNTAIN

If we are truly universal, then where is our home and who is our family? These are the questions we ask as we begin to notice that perhaps we are not like the others living their daily lives. The questions we ask are bigger than we know, so the answers are only revealed to us equal to our ability to understand and our willingness to receive them. Often through our research, we will find a checklist that will identify us with others like us. We find community, and we feel not quite so alone, until one day we realize that we are and always have been at home.

There comes a point in time when we learn that "being" is the ultimate experience of our existence. While we exist within our physical bodies, the idea of being and existing as energy is a foreign concept. Our physical bodies allow us to do, play, run, work, and experience pleasure and pain. That in itself offers simple pleasure, but then we remember that we are more than our physical forms. We are energy, and our physical bodies do not contain that energy. As much as 90 percent of the energy that we exist as exists outside our physical bodies. You have heard that we only use about 10 percent of our brains? That is because the majority of our brains are used for our connection to the energy outside our physical presence. We are primarily energy, and as such, we are forces of nature that are as powerful as we choose to remember ourselves to be.

Though I learned and realized that I was connected to energy beyond this place and time, I did not understand why I was so alone in this knowledge.

Why is this knowledge so uncommon when this truth has existed throughout history? When learning anything new, we always enjoy sharing it with others, yet once we are on the path of learning about our own power and true existence, we quickly move to the leading edge. As a result, we run out of research topics, and we run out of people who have already experienced what we have. We then have to rely on our own senses of what we are experiencing to be true and real. We shift from attractors of matching experiences to our thoughts and desires to creating our experiences. We become creators and accept the full responsibility of our actions.

When we become creators by understanding our power, we consciously use our thoughts and desires to give way to whole new expansion and experiences. We eventually become teachers because as we expand further than what is presently known we become the ones who will light the path for others to follow. We move from servitude, the "have to do's" in life, to being in service to others by sharing our knowledge and insights of places others have not yet gone. This is what the story of returning home with the elixir describes in Joseph Campbell's *The Hero's Journey*. Campbell, an American mythologist and writer, identified what he called a "monomyth." The Hero's Journey, both an internal and external journey of expansion and experience, is our one human story of triumph and tragedy, wisdom and ignorance, bliss and despair, and union and separation. What we have conquered, we now have to learn to live with. This is when our true work, our purpose, begins, and in most cases, it is a time when true loneliness sets in. There is no going back to pretending we are "normal." Our expansion swallowed the path we came in on as if it were lost to a newly closed black hole.

My life-coach-turned-spiritual-teacher told me that one day soon I would surpass my need for her guidance. I did not believe it at the time. A year later, during one of our sessions, I found her giving me less guidance and more reassurance of the answers and understanding I was receiving on my own.

In the evenings while walking my dogs, I would search the stars and feel an ache of being left here alone. The question lingered: What was I here to do? I still did not know. Sometimes the feeling became so overwhelming that tears would sting my eyes and form a lump in my throat as if I were a child lost in a busy mall.

Memories would flood into my mind about my childhood and the men who pushed me beyond my years. Perhaps it was to give me the strength to endure this time in my life when I truly did feel lost. A specific time from my childhood often came to mind. I was fishing with my father and grandfather on the banks of the Missouri River when two teenagers dressed in the typical bellbottoms and big hair of the early seventies came to ask for some worms in exchange for a few beers.

My grandfather sent me alone with them to the other side of the river to collect payment. At the time, I was aware that sending a small child alone with strangers was not a good idea, but I went anyway. As I followed the teens over the bridge, I saw that they were obviously annoyed by my presence. They stopped when we reached a point on the bridge where they could jump down from the road to the riverbank on the other side. As I peered down, pondering whether I could make the same jump, they never looked up, and I decided the drop was too big for me.

They did not seem to notice that I was no longer following them. Feeling mad at grandfather for sending me, I walked alone to the end of the bridge. As I began to make my way back toward the bank, I had to navigate around a small pond that was full of croaking bullfrogs jumping all around me. I was terrified and angry. There were thick vines and weeds that grabbed and pierced my clothing. My anger with the boys and my grandfather turned to frustration with myself for being too afraid to jump, thus leading to my precarious situation. My father eventually found me entangled in the vines, inching my way toward the direction of the riverbank, and asked me what I was doing — as if it was a journey I had chosen on my own. Scratched, scraped, muddy, and tearful, I let him lead me out of the vines to a path around the pond and trees that I had not seen from my small perspective.

Every experience we have brings wisdom and knowledge for the future. The fact that the memory of that day emerged so often for me told me I was facing the same challenge again. I was on my own, negotiating entanglements that were more in my mind than physical, but they were just as scary and real.

The truth is, despite how wonderful my life was, I wanted to be rescued again. I wanted to stop being fearful of being alone. I wanted to have the ease and grace I knew was possible but was unseen to me from my physical viewpoint. I was angry that I was left on this planet with masses of unaware people living day in and day out bitching, complaining, and worrying about everything and nothing at all.

I was exhausted by the contrast and conflict that forced me to live in a reality I did not believe in. I was consciously aware that this was not an existence that was necessary, but I could not find my way through the day without being witness to the constant battle for survival. Where was the thriving? Where was the ability to live our lives in joy? I didn't feel I could even muster the emotion of joy in this battleground of density, of made-up rules and untruths disguised as politics, religion, and morals.

I could feel in my very soul that our physical technology was Stone Age compared to how we were able to communicate and create in the nonphysical realm. I wanted to peel the skin off my body and be free again, to exist in ease and harmony with All That Is. I hated our best form of communication and the processes it took to run and maintain our computers and smartphones.

Why could others not hear my thoughts as I could hear theirs? Worse yet, why were people completely unaware, and why did they seemingly not care, that there was an easier way to live their lives? Why did they turn their backs on who they truly were and embrace being victims of their circumstances? Why could I see their divinity, their light, and who they came to be, but I could not see my own? I was stuck here living in this dense, thick, low-vibrating energy while they — my family, all the facets of the Universe — were out there in the stars loving me, watching me, looking over me, and feeling what I felt. Alas, I could only sense them.

This small, almost intangible sense of a family somewhere beyond here was the only thread that kept my soul alive. I was stuck somewhere between here and the stars. There was a time when I wanted to jump just like that little girl on the bridge, but something held me back just as it had then. I came to understand it was my children who firmly held me here on this planet. It was the fact that they chose me to be their mother that motivated me to continue waking up every day, involving myself in the heavy, thick entanglement of real life.

Just one year before, something happened to me that is nearly beyond words to describe that showed me our true power and potential as humans. Yet again, on the outside, it seemed to everyone else I was happy and had the perfect life, but the truth was I missed the ease and grace of the nonphysical so much that misery radiated through my soul. Most of my waking time was spent with the thought of leaving this plane of existence. Something seemed to have gone terribly wrong with the intention of this being a physical playground for the nonphysical. One night after a fight with my partner, I stormed into my backyard and screamed at the dusk of the night, "Get me off of this FUCKING planet NOW!" I collapsed onto my knees in utter surrender.

Without warning, something happened. In front of me, shimmering like a mirage in the desert, a portal opened, glowing with golden yellow and orange loving light. Had I done it? They heard me. The pure, raw emotion of my soul created something I did not know was possible. It was true: Portals exist, and one was before me. I did not fully understand it at the time, but my desire to peel off this earthly body was so sincere and so intense that I created the possibility of leaving and vanishing without a trace.

The portal shimmered in front of me, and an energy being emerged and spoke to me through my mind: "It is okay. You can come now." The voice was gentle and so full of love beyond what I have felt before. It was a love I wanted desperately to feel, but rather than relief or joy, fear gripped me in that moment. I intuitively knew that it was real. Teetering on the brink between disappearing and staying, my desire to step forward into the portal filled every cell in my body with pure wanting, but I could not step forward. My children inside the house held me in place. What would my sons do without me? Who would they become if I left? How could I ever leave them? I couldn't, not ever.

Just as fast as it appeared, it was gone. My heart had made my choice. My sons were the reason I was here. They were the reason I lived through my horrible divorce, and they were the reason I came into this world. In that moment, I knew my reason for being here and that it was ultimately my choice to remain.

That experience gave me a newfound awareness that allowed me the privilege of seeing everything with new eyes. I had a new feeling of connectedness, almost as if there was more than me seeing through my physical eyes. It was as if I now existed in a symbiotic relationship with the whole Universe and the Universe was using my eyes to witness life in physical form. Everything around me, every conversation and every interaction, now seemed to be something I was consciously retaining in my memory for me to remember and for them — my soul family and all the facets of All That Is — to experience.

Learning that it was my choice to live in this state, not fully present on Earth or in the stars, caught somewhere between the two, made the pain more bearable than what I felt before. It seemed that the only reason I was here was to experience this place in this time and to be with my sons. So I stopped reading the posts and blogs I was feverishly studying. I had my answers, I knew my power, and I knew that I was not alone.

For years I had been reading books and blogs, and I grew impatient with all the negativity about the government, Illuminati, and secret societies enslaving, poisoning, and killing. I knew there was some truth in the information, but focusing on any negative situation was only creating more fear and negativity. I knew the speculation that aliens were coming to save us before the poles shifted at the end of the Mayan calendar was not true. I realized that instead of waiting for a savior, we needed to awaken to the fact that we were the ones who could save ourselves.

Our thoughts create our realities. Our beliefs are the basis for how we perceive life. We are powerful — so powerful that if we believe enough, we can walk off this planet without dying. If I awakened to this knowing, I knew that everyone else could if they chose to.

• • •

One day while browsing through books in Barnes & Noble, I found myself in the historical fiction section. At one point in my life, I was an avid book reader. I especially liked authors who were able to bring a fictional story to life through accurate historical details. History, religion, and the arts were always my favorite subjects; however, over the recent years, I had only read spiritual subjects and science blogs pertaining to truth seekers. As my eyes skimmed over the titles of each book, I mentally checked off many of the stories of English queens, courts, and commoners that I already read, and then my eyes fell on a thick, plain-looking binding. The title was *The Outlander* by Diana Gabaldon.

I was more intrigued by the thickness of the book and the thought of losing myself in its pages than I was by the title, so I pulled it off the shelf. The story was about an American woman, Claire Beauchamp, who time-traveled through a portal in the standing stones of Scotland in the early 1700s, where she met an outlaw named Jamie Fraser. The reviews on the back of the book spoke about the author's accuracy with historical detail.

The Outlander included the history of the Jacobite Rebellion, which I had heard of but really knew nothing about. I smiled when I realized that this book incorporated the best of the two worlds I enjoyed. I was intrigued by how the author could mix the two and have such positive, prestigious reviews. I was sold. The best part was if I liked the book, there was a whole series I could lose myself in.

Over the next year, I replaced my knowledge seeking with the story of Jamie and Claire as I consumed book after book. I fell in love with Jamie for the way he loved, protected, accepted, supported, and believed in Claire. I identified with Claire, a lone woman trying to find her way during a time when no one understood her knowledge of the future. My heart opened just as hers did to a man, a country, and a life that was harder than she knew it had to be. I, like Claire, thought my knowledge and understanding were not magical but rather just not yet experienced by everyone.

As I read every detail about the history and relationship that unfolded in the series, it occurred to me that these two souls came from the same place. They lived in different times, yet the Universe stepped in and conspired to bring them together. Their differences were obvious, but their hearts were one. They lived to love and to serve the greater good of humanity, which compelled them through choices that would tear them apart, break their bodies and spirits, and bring them back together again and again. I devoured each book and lived through the characters' tragedies, hardships, and impossibilities with them, knowing that when they found each other again they would be healed and find joy despite their circumstances. I wondered whether they were twin flames.

There are many theories about twin flames — how we recognize them and call them forth. Many who study the subject believe that your twin flame is your soul's exact vibrational match *but* also your polar opposite. They believe that the soul splits into the feminine and masculine, each going forth and expanding.

I knew I hadn't met my twin flame, and I found myself beginning to doubt his existence here on Earth. I learned to communicate with All That Is in an open and clear dialogue, very much like author Neale Donald Walsch did when he wrote *Conversations with God*. I often would ask questions about twin flames and soul mates and wait for the answers. The answers always surprised me because they were so different from the information I learned from others who wrote about these topics.

The answers from my questions told me twin flames come from the first expansion of our souls. Each soul is created from a universal desire to experience. When a soul is created, it is the highest form of the energy of love that expands until it breaks into two. This first split, or expansion, is the twin flame. The expansion then continues, much like we know it happens during the creation of our physical experience, and with each subsequent expansion, it becomes more specific in its purpose.

This is how we know that we are One. We are merely the expansion of desire and focused intention. Energetically, we are as complete as All That Is, as God. The physical clothes, or skins, we choose to wear separate us from others by giving us containers for our energy to experience separateness. It is only when we reunite with All That Is that we can see who we are: one in all forms.

Until this time, we are valued for our experiences while utilizing contrast to awaken our desire for further understanding. We often suffer, not realizing that we have chosen this for our own knowing. When our questions and intentions change and become focused on love, on who we are, and on why we are here, we eventually begin to meet ourselves in various forms. We then recognize the ache we carry inside us is for our twin. Our twins then become the Holy Grail that we search for because only they can show us the whole truth of our divinity.

Very few twins have come together on Earth's physical plane. I believe Jesus and Mary Magdalene were two who did and that the story of Jesus as most of us have been taught is not the whole truth. I believe the early church masked most of the testaments that spoke of Jesus and Mary's union and the ascension that was finally created through their twin flame union. In recognizing the power of this union, those who were in positions of power sought to hide the information. They believed that the shift in the Christ consciousness created by Jesus and Mary would weaken their position of power. They were correct to be fearful, for the union between the two changed the world far beyond what could have been imagined at the time.

Twin souls, or twin flames, are mirrors of the soul. Often their wounds are the same. Their weaknesses reflect each other. Their strengths radiate as one. The contrast we experience on the exterior is no longer present, because this final connection is the healing of what lies within. This describes Jamie and Claire's union in every way throughout the Outlander series

It is often speculated that there are false twins — twins who are close but not real twins, who seem to align in so many ways yet their relationship can sometimes become destructive. There are many who believe that, in some cases, twins run away from the intensity of the experience of meeting someone so close to the vibrational frequency of their own souls. Perhaps seeing the clarity of their own reflection in another is what frightens people.

These believers say that the twins will eventually come back together either in this lifetime or the next. It is a common belief that twins do not have the romantic exterior relationship that we all dream of as children but instead form relationships that are challenging because of the power and energy that is brought forth when the twin souls meet. I agree with this idea, yet our desire to meet our twins is a force that I believe drives all creation. I believe that while the pieces of our souls expand, they feel the absence of the whole we knew we were at one point when our souls were created. The emptiness we feel deep within is what continuously drives us toward expansion, but it is not until we begin to expand within ourselves that we begin our journey home to our twins. This is the new path we must create to return to where we once began.

In the books, I could see that neither Jamie nor Claire ran from each other because of the union. I could see that the were true twin flames rather than false twins despite the fact they endured great suffering in staying together. Jamie and Claire had alway felt the emptiness in their souls that was only eased by the awareness of the other. They were indeed twin flames.

When I finished the last book of the series about Jamie and Claire, I wondered if I could call forth my twin. Could his energy join me in the here and now, even if it existed in another time and place? Did I actually want to call him forth? I had found such wonderful peace over the past years just being alone, reading, walking my dogs, loving my cats, and relishing in my sons' victories on the soccer field. I lived in joy now and actually felt whole as one person. My life was actually perfect! The thought of changing it was insanity. I realized that I became the Buddha on the mountain; I was one with all. I was in bliss just being. What more could a person ask for?

CHAPTER FOUR

FROM STUDENT TO TEACHER TO STUDENT

I was sitting in a dark theater on a weekday watching Julia Roberts's character collide with a man on a bicycle in Bali shaking my head. "No, no, no," I thought. I cried as the movie ended with the "girl always ends up with the guy" fairy tale. Why do they always have to sail away into a "happily ever after" sunset? Does that ever happen in real life? She worked so hard and had been through so much to find her peace! Why did she want to give that up to be with some guy? Eat, Pray, Love, *the title echoed in my head, and within a week, my profile was on Match.com.*

I found it — the peace we all seek, the bliss we all want. I found the joy in a moment echoing, reverberating, in every cell as I watched a heron soar across the lake behind my office or when I spoke to strangers passing by. Why is it that others want what you have created in your life and, at the same time, they desire to change what you want? I no sooner asked the question, "What more could a person ask for than what I have now?" than I was slapped in the face with the answer.

When the book *Eat, Pray, Love* by Elizabeth Gilbert came out, many people told me I should read it. I might have considered reading it if they had not told me, "She is just like you." I found earlier in my life that every time someone told me I was "just like" someone else, I was usually not happy with the comparison.

My best friend in art school, Caresse, compared me to Rose from *Golden Girls* because I apparently told too many Missouri stories in college. Other comparisons included Woody Allen's Annie Hall (which still befuddles me), Dharma from the TV show *Dharma and Greg* (I guess because I'm more spiritual and quirky than others), and Lauren Graham from *Gilmore Girls* (for both her looks and attitude). In my opinion, all these women seemed a bit off, yet with each example, I could see hints that may have rung true for me.

So the idea of reading a book about a woman who hated her perfect life, got divorced, and traveled to Italy to eat pasta only to end up in an ashram not speaking to anyone before she found herself in Bali, rang a little too close to home for me to want to go down that path. What they failed to tell me was that she ended up sailing away *supposedly* happily ever after.

I sat there as the credits rolled down the movie screen ticked off and annoyed that a perfectly good movie ended with the idea that I should lose my balance to find my balance. I did not see anything wrong with the idea of being at one with myself.

The Universe gives us messages in ways we are not expecting. I know that if we do not listen, then we usually get hit harder the next time with the same message. That did not necessarily seem appealing. So I rolled my eyes to the ceiling and cursed the fact that once you see something, like your parents having sex, it can never be unseen. Somehow, watching the movie's ending had felt just as uncomfortable and inerasable.

I was just as annoyed with the reason I was seeing the movie as I was with the ending of it. My advertising agency expertise was in destination marketing and tourism. Over the years, we were recognized for our emotional work and its ability to create action and increase the economic impact for our clients. However, one of our destinations had a new marketing director, and we had to go through the process of waiting for her "aha!" moment. In this case, our client found *Eat, Pray, Love* to be her moment — when she realized that flashy banners and price points were not what people were truly looking for in their lives. I should have been grateful that she was finally coming around, but the movie felt too personal for me to summon the gratitude of her awakening.

I was on the same journey that Julia Roberts's character took. I knew what it was to feel what she felt — to have the perfect life that was crushing the life out of my soul. I had sat on the bathroom floor begging God for answers. I had given away everything for the boys and my freedom. I had a crazy, unexpected, momentary relationship with deep meaning but little stability after my divorce. I immersed myself in the experience of my senses. I meditated for hours, searching for answers until I found them. What I didn't do was travel the world while doing all of that. I should have planned better so that I too could have seen the world while finding myself. However, I did understand the deeper meaning of the movie and why the Universe conspired for me to see it, because it obviously was not about the marketing for our account.

• • •

One of two things happens when you ask stupid questions of the Universe. Either you receive the answer and are guided by inspiration, or you ignore the answer and get beaten up until you are ready to give in, beg for mercy, and eventually get your ass into action. I am smart enough to know I asked for this in one way or another, so that evening I had a serious talk with God.

It went something like this: "God, if I were to consider this 'happily ever after' idea again, then he better take my breath away — I mean *really* wow me — in order to make it worthwhile for me to lose what I have gained, the peace in my life that I love. I am no longer looking for contrast, lessons, and someone who does not get me."

When I finished my statement of criteria, it occurred to me why I had watched so many back-to-back episodes of *The Millionaire Matchmaker*, even though I was not looking for a guy. I knew exactly to do. I searched my heart for the five non-negotiable things I wanted in a companion. I got as far as "tall, spiritual, a father," and then I drew a blank. What did I really want? There was no answer. I rolled the question around in my head for days. Who could sweep me off my feet? Who would be worth it? I started to panic because the answers that usually came to me so easily were not showing up. It was as if I were unplugged from the Universe. What the hell happened? Where were my answers?

Every once in a while, something happens to people when they are about to have a spiritual breakthrough. It is called the dark night of the soul. It is a time when you must dig deeper than you have ever imagined and listen with new awareness. It happens when the Universe has changed the frequency at which it is speaking to us. We must raise our vibrations and elevate our beings to match that frequency to get the answers. I have always believed the forty days and forty nights Jesus spent in the desert were this very thing. Can you imagine facing death and losing your connection to All That Is just before you walk your path?

My experience was not exactly comparable, but I also felt as if I were facing certain death. I knew that I was about to lose who I had come to know as me. It was this fear that had kept me separated from what I grew to trust and rely on, which was my connection. That is when I knew: I just wanted to find *me* again.

Opening my heart to the Universe, I said these words out loud: "I am looking for me. I want my twin flame. That's what I am looking for." Yes, that was it. I wanted a reflection of my soul. That was it. I did not need a list because I knew who I was. I felt peace once again, and I went to sleep satisfied that I had figured it out.

The next morning I bounced into the office with a plan. I was going to "call in" my twin flame. I was not sure how I was going to do it, but once you have a plan, the Universe responds rather quickly. What I was not prepared for was how quickly.

Being forty and single had not been sitting well with my friends and staff. So when I made a passing comment that afternoon that perhaps I would consider looking for someone I could "sail off with," as the movie suggested, everyone went into action. Being at an advertising agency, you can only imagine how quickly an ad can be whipped up for a desperate, lonely single mom who is looking for someone to take her out of her misery.

What was even more amusing (or possibly frightening) than my staff's quick action were the variations of copy and photos that were selected by my "matchmakers." My business partner selected a bare-shouldered shot of me taken from above at an awards banquet. I was wearing blood-red lipstick to disguise a fever-induced, pasty-white zombie look. Her copy suggested that I needed a conservative, nice man who had a job.

My senior art director, who was an expert in online dating, wrote an ad full of chat room abbreviations: "Spiritual DWF ISO DWM w/ GSOH." I had no idea what that meant, but apparently it's a secret code for experienced daters. I only later learned it meant "spiritual divorced white female in search of divorced white male with great sense of humor" — which was true, but I doubted what I was really looking for had an accompanying set of initials. He also provided me with a sophisticated professional photo to ensure I would get inquiries from professionals.

My beloved friend and accountant, Deana, picked a more relaxed photo of me taken in California the previous year. What she liked about the photo was it had been taken from a distance showing how thin I was. Deana's ad said that I loved sushi, Italian food, and laughing. This was also true, but I was looking for something much deeper than any typical description that can be put into words. With my choices before me, it occurred to me that this might be harder than I thought.

Later that night, I joined Match.com. I created a profile that told the truth. It started something like this: "You know the movie *Eat, Pray, Love*? That's me, but I did not travel to Italy, India, and Bali. I took my own journey while managing a business, two sons as a single mom, and five furry critters as my companions. I am not seeking contrast; I am looking for someone who gets what I mean by that, who is tall, a divorced father, and a soul living in a human body." I used every photo my friends selected, and then I saved the profile and went to bed.

I have since learned from my male friends that it is not typical for men to receive an inbox full of emails after joining a site like Match.com, but it is typical for women. If you have never tried an online dating site, I should warn you to never sip hot coffee when checking your inbox for the first time. Perhaps I should have felt excited as I mopped up the spilled coffee from my keyboard, but I was more intimidated by than appreciative of all the responses. I got this sinking feeling that took a hold of my body as I read through the various messages and strange offers. If I wasn't interested, I would respond as politely as possible to each person who had messaged me. While I was doing this, I received a message back from someone I had disqualified. The message was downright unfriendly, and it shocked me: "Well, bitch, I would not want to go out with your snooty ass anyway. Good luck finding your sugar daddy!" What? Wow! Somebody needed to do some healing work! Thank God I didn't consider him.

I began browsing profiles that the site considered matches for me, and I started to wonder if every man in southwest Florida golfed, fished, and drove motorcycles. The funny thing was, I never noticed motorcycles on the road. Were all these pictures of them with their dream bikes staged? All golfers were crossed out immediately. I was a golf widow once, and I knew to avoid pitting myself against the calling of nineteen holes and a clubhouse full of cold beer. On the other hand, fishing was the only thing I considered worse than golfing. These were time-intensive hobbies that I did not want to compete with.

I moved on. Delete, delete, delete. I felt bad, but I didn't want to meet any of these men. As I drained my coffee and inbox, my business partner came in to see what was up for the day. I directed her to my computer with a head nod. Her delight that I created a profile on Match.com turned from a grin into a grimace when she saw the options saved on my screen. Apparently, she was not looking for a tall, handsome free spirit for me.

She sighed and asked to see my profile. I gave her my password, and then I left for my morning appointment. When I returned, I learned that she had decided that I needed to reach out to more appropriate choices, and she found just the one. After all this time, I still laugh at the "perfect" man she chose for me. I read the description she pulled up and then asked if her husband finally gave up on her and joined Match. I loved her husband, Matt, and that's who her perfect man online sounded like; however, this was not the man I was looking for.

A few hours later, the one I was looking for sent me a message. His name was Adam. I read his profile: a single dad of two sons, six foot three, blue-eyed, guitar playing, spiritual warrior looking for the One. My heart was immediately filled with joy and gratitude. Grinning ear to ear, I shared his profile with everyone over lunch. Undaunted by everyone else's expressions of concern, I typed out a reply to him and hit "send." We exchanged a few messages, and before I knew it, I was on the phone listening to his Boston accent and planning our first date. As I hung up the phone, I thought, "Oh my! This could be worth it!"

Have you ever been in a situation in which you haven't seen your best friend for years, yet when you get back together again, you marvel at how he or she looks exactly the same, and you pick up exactly where you left off? That's how I felt when I met Adam a.k.a. Mr. Match. I instantly gave him a big hug when I got out of my car, as if we were long-lost friends.

Did I mention that I hadn't dated in years? Wait a moment … did I say "years"? Maybe I should say that I hadn't been on a first date in decades. The relationships I did have I just happened to fall into rather than starting at the beginning with a traditional first date. I had no reference for what to expect — other than the typical first-date horror stories I'd heard over the years.

Incredibly, our date did not feel like a date at all. It was more like a reunion of people who had shared significant experiences together. We ordered a few drinks and an appetizer and sat at the bar, intently validating everything we both had learned throughout our spiritual journeys. Even when they're drunk, people are attracted to the light of a positive connection, so we should not have been surprised to find that, as the hours flew by, a crowd of eavesdropping patrons had surrounded us. They were listening intently to things they surely needed to hear and were basking in the reflected brilliance of our magical connection.

When we did manage to break the spell and notice our new friends, the feeling of claustrophobia engulfed both of us. It was time to go. However, the evening could not end so abruptly — or so easily. We both needed more confirmation, connection, and time.

When we arrived at my house (I know, stupid, right?), I poured us both a glass of wine. I handed one glass to Adam and curled up next to him on the couch, admiring his presence. He exuded strength and sureness, and his essence was of someone familiar. As we talked, he leaned over to kiss me. I knew it was time to tell him that "this" was *not* going to happen.

It had been years since I'd slept with anyone. Not because it wasn't possible, but because it was my body, and I owned it — all of it. I came to see my body as a sacred chalice of the Divine Feminine. As an open vessel to God, the purity of my vibration was something I cherished and refused to randomly give away. If I were ever to unite with another, it was going to be magical, not physical. Not to mention my connection to All That Is was still lost, and without it, I was not using my body just for physical satisfaction.

I wanted the first time I slept with a man again to be on a mountaintop with leaves falling all around us. I wanted it to be perfect. I was going to wait for the perfect situation, despite the appeal of this tall, handsome, and intoxicating man on my sofa who kissed me like he knew what he was doing. My mind was set, and as I began pulling away from his kiss, it happened.

The dark night of my soul ended, and I began getting a lecture on perfection. Yep, the Universe stepped in right in the middle of everything, and I clearly heard a voice say, "Perfection is not about a mountaintop. Perfection is about being love, love overflowing and pouring into another. Love is perfection, not a place."

The instant connection stopped me in my tracks. Having been clairaudient all my life, I was used to "hearing" insight in this way. I had learned how to distinguish my thoughts from the voices of guides. What I considered a gift, others saw as a reason to put someone in a padded room. So I never shared where my information came from. I privately relied on the guidance I received, and when it was not around, I felt lost. However, guidance does not come in our preferred timing or with our preferred choice of wisdom. This guidance was clear and not at all what I expected.

Answering this guided insight with my thoughts, I asked, "Now you show up? Can't you tell I am in the middle of something?" As I watched Mr. Match's eyebrows furrow, looking at me having this untimely conversation with myself, I thought, "Well, surely this is over now. He thinks you are crazy, Kimberly."

Despite my distraction, the guidance continued: "Love can only expand when it is experienced on every level. You are human — a divine human."

Yes, I was human, and the sensation of his body touching mine awakened something I lost long ago. Desire was something that hadn't crossed my mind in a long time, but with my guidance assuring me that all was well, coupled with the synchronicity of this man's presence, I let myself succumb to the pleasure of him. I could tell he was confused but not willing to say no, either, so he let me lead. I became a physical, emotional, and spiritual expression of love. I say that because I am not clear about what happened, but I was never so confident, so open, so full of fire, and so full of love. It had nothing to do with him, actually. It felt as though he had just shown up to assist a human becoming a divine physical being.

I sent him home a few hours later, and I laid outside staring into the heavens for a long time before going to bed. When I woke the next morning, I wasn't thinking of Mr. Match. I was thinking, "What the hell happened?" Of course, he called and sent a few text messages, but he more or less was asking the same thing I was: What was that?

I wondered, "Is this what happens when you meet a twin flame? Is this the experience they talk about?" I did not know the answer, and I was not getting anything from above, so I went to the only place I knew for sure would have answers: Google.

I typed into the search box one of the few things I had never researched on the topic of twin flames — "sex with a twin flame" — and hit enter. The next thing I knew, I was reading about the very experience I'd just had. "You make instant tantric love" is what caught my eye. I'd heard about tantric sex before and was lucky enough to have experienced it, but it had not been like this. What I had just experienced was an instant kundalini awakening. The rising of the kundalini energy, which lies dormant in our lower spines, can become awakened over long periods of practice. When an individual can open the flow of his or her energy through the chakra vortexes and finally allow the kundalini energy to extend up through the crown chakra, then he or she has achieved enlightenment. What I had actually done was opened myself to the divine, connecting myself to the universal energy stream, and experienced a glimpse of enlightenment. And it had been bliss, a kind of bliss that somehow filled that deep ache, the one I had known my whole life. The author of the blog noted, "If you experienced an instant awakening by having sex with your twin flame, God help you." Really? That is the advice someone is giving? What did that mean?

Responding to Adam's text asking what had happened, I promised that the experience was not "normal" for me either. But I did some research, and I wanted to share it with him. I put the links together and sent him an email. The response I got surprised me. He seemed almost jealous. As deep and spiritual as he was, he had never experienced anything like that night, but after reading the information I shared with him, he felt he had missed something for himself. I wondered, if we were twin flames, wouldn't we have shared the experience?

Adam left for a few days to go to Boston, where he spends the summer with his sons every year. While he was away, we exchanged a few emails and photos. I was very much at peace with the situation. More importantly, the kundalini awakening began transforming me in ways I never imagined possible. I felt I had a deeper compassion for everything I witnessed. What was unique was that this new deeper compassion for everything never caused pain or worry. Instead, a heart connection grew to everything I experienced. I began to feel honored to be a part of life and all of humanity. And I now was able to manifest with a mere passing thought.

As I did more research, I came across more information on theories of twins being our polar opposites. I could see this in Adam as time went on. Although we never went on another date, we became friends. I began noticing that we seemed to be on the same vibrational frequency yet saw things from opposite viewpoints. As we each evolved and studied nearly the same topics, I began to see he saw everything in an darker light. Where he saw conspiracy and control, I saw focus and experience. Although we tried to make time to get back together, it seemed as if we were not magnets but rather opposites, pushing against each other around the same DNA helix. It was as if we were a reversed reflection of each other. As we evolved higher and higher in our vibrations, it was as if the *one* time Adam and I came together in such an instant attraction that we had been struck by something creating distance rather than coming together as twins would. In science class, I learned that when you strike two magnets in just the right way, they will repel each other, and Adam and I were now repelling each other.

CHAPTER FIVE

ONE TO THE SECOND POWER

Often when it appears nothing at all is happening, that is when everything is actually happening. When everything seems to be falling apart, it is actually rebuilding. As we grow our spiritual roots and branches, our exteriors must change — what I call the molting. It is like a snake shedding its skin. It can be painless or painful, depending only on our own need to keep the skin we have become accustomed to.

While Adam and I were busy repelling each other, my work began to change dramatically. In May of 2010, the British Petroleum disaster began filling the Gulf of Mexico with oil. As the media continued to project the path that the oil would take, the tourism industry on the Gulf Coast of Florida was in a panic. Ninety percent of my clients were on the Gulf Coast, and the outlook was not positive. Our funding relied on the bed tax that was collected by the hotels, and with visitors choosing other destinations, answers and funding were now at a minimum.

Although my internal existence was expanding, my external existence was shrinking. My business partner left the business. I fought my way out of a five-year lease and moved my office into my home while shifting my employees into remote subcontractors connected through technology.

Only because I was enlightened to the truth, that we create our own realities, my view of what was happening was not that of panic or terror as it might have been years before. Instead, I knew that a huge change on the outside was needed to align with what was happening on the inside. So rather than think, "Why did this happen to me?" I welcomed the changes, believing they were for my highest good.

Tourism advertising and marketing had beaten me up over the years. My passion for driving economies was stifled by power and politics. The awards that lined our walls lost their meaning, and I knew this feeling would result in one of two things: (1) If I was unwilling to evolve, I would receive more of the same misery, or (2) I could embrace the change and trust the Universe to bring new and exciting opportunities for me to follow.

I chose the latter. How it was going to turn out, I was not sure. Before I moved my business home, the work to create a new reality had already begun. I knew that by announcing to the Universe what my intentions were and taking action steps to allow it to happen, it would work.

I began thinking and envisioning how to market in a new way. I asked myself, "What is the next big thing in marketing?" I knew I wanted to create a mastermind group that would set an intention of calling in customers for our clients. I wondered if it was possible to use the concept of manifestation as a marketing method. However, I needed a way to monitor the return on investment, because that would be key to selling the program. And I needed to know the time it would take to achieve the results we wanted. Universal and practical measurable time conversion had never been truly reliable for me before, but I needed to find a way to understand it if I was going to get this off the ground. I discussed this with friends and colleagues, all of whom seemed to think I'd lost my mind.

I knew the campaigns and brands I created over the years were always on the leading edge. Implementing a new direction of marketing or new look of campaigns before others could see the direction the market was heading was my strength — and part of the reason I was frustrated with marketing as a whole. My older clients trusted my instincts and were always rewarded with the results. The newer, less-experienced marketing directors, the "I have a master's degree in marketing and two years of practical experience" clients, relied on proof that something had already worked for a computer before they were brave enough to risk trying something new. They were not leaders and not interested in the leading edge.

My philosophy, however, was to always be brave enough to go beyond what was already proven to be true. I outgrew the set of people I was working with, and my new partners were nowhere to be found yet, so it was time I started to live by my own words.

Visualize, feel, and act as if what you want is already true and you have already received what you desire. That is the basis of manifestation. It seemed obvious to me that I would have to manifest the reality I wanted to live because it didn't seem to exist yet. Being alone in my office the majority of the time, I was able to have open conversations with myself. My dogs never minded, as I would discuss how we would serve our clients, sell, and market the new business. I even visualized a partner to do it with me. He was tall, handsome, single, and intuitive, but he had a different skill set than I did. He was European minded and had been in business for many years.

He also believed it was time to bring awareness to a new way of doing business. I would have pretend conversations with clients, telling them what my role was in this new company. "I am a seer," I would explain. In Asia, most companies already have this person employed. "My role is like an advisor, much like Deanna Troi was to Captain Picard in *Star Trek: The Next Generation*. I am able to telepathically communicate and understand the needs and situations of others as I assist leaders to create positive outcomes."

One day, as I was having one of these conversations between getting my traditional marketing work done and acting as if my future already existed, I realized that I was not just talking. I was hearing too. I was now in a dialogue with someone who didn't even exist, at least not in physical form. The most fascinating part was I realized he was giving me the process of how this was all coming about and how it would eventually come into existence. It was the voice of Jamie from the Outlander book series, the man I had gotten to know so well and loved dearly for the person he chose to be.

I began openly "hearing" the partner I was manifesting all the time, and not just regarding the work I was creating. Although I was used to being able to communicate with the other side, I was aware that the conversations I was having with a being I could not see were pretend (much like preparing for a speech). But this new relationship seemed more real than not.

Sometimes when I was cooking, he would ask me if I needed a spice I didn't even know I had in the pantry. His voice would randomly remind me to get something at the store that I didn't know I needed, only to arrive home and discover that he was right. I began discussing everything with him, from how to take care of an issue with the kids to how I should handle my clients.

Even though I could speak to the other side, I'd never had this kind of dialogue with such clarity and frequency. I became so fond of him, so comfortable, that I literally could feel the physical presence of his energy. This relationship felt so real; the thought of the physical man walking up and talking as if we already knew each other seemed probable. I half expected to hear his human voice behind me one day, and I began to become acutely aware that I would soon meet my partner who I knew was also my twin flame.

The bird messengers started making their presence known to me again, starting with a red female cardinal that tapped on my window every day. Cardinals give us the understanding that life is eternal, and they often bring messages from the other side. I fell into a space of peace, knowing that I was consciously creating the reality I so badly desired.

During one morning meditation, I asked my beloved invisible partner how I would recognize him when I met him. What I was expecting to see was an image of a tall, handsome man wearing something I would be able to identify. Instead, I could only see a glimpse of his eyes.

One afternoon, my father asked me about my dating status and what had happened with Adam. I briefly explained that he had his own issues to take care of and that I was waiting for the One — who I was meant to be with. He shot back an obvious question: "How will you know when you meet him that he is the One?"

My answer came out of nowhere, surprising both of us: "He will be a modern-day smuggler, a guy who would go to any lengths to help his family — like Jamie in *The Outlander*."

My dad was an avid reader, and I gave him the first book of the series to read. He thought Jamie was a great character. He liked that he was someone who loved his wife because of her uniqueness. He knew this was the kind of man I would need in my life to make me happy, and more than anything, he wished for me to have the happiness my soul ached for.

Everywhere I went, I searched for the eyes I had seen. They were a deep-sea blue with hints of emerald green, and they reflected light as the crest of a wave might. But they were nowhere to be found. I began calling in his energy through my deep meditations. I could see him filling into a physical body cell by cell. He was tall, handsome, strong, funny, and kind. He was a man's man.

I knew that the purpose of twins coming together was to bring forth the Christ consciousness, but I believed that there was more to it than that. I understood that our twin flames were to assist with our ascension. I believed that our twins were to help us do what has never been done in the physical plane before now, at least not on a mass scale. I believed that now, in this place and time, we are able to fully ascend into our complete divine essences with full awareness of our whole existence while living in physical form. My brief experience with Adam awakened me to the essence of my divine being — of being a goddess and human at the same time.

I wondered whether others believed it was possible to fully ascend within our physical bodies. I sometimes wondered whether Christ had died to ascend or that maybe he actually ascended before he died. Or was it possible there was more truth to the idea that he actually did not die at all, but lived, and if he did live, did he actually achieve ascension? Was this truly the Christ consciousness living as an ascended human?

Was it possible that the Catholic Church knew this all along and hid this information from the masses? Was human ascension what was written about on the missing Dead Sea Scrolls? Is it possible that somewhere deep in the Vatican vaults, this truth is hiding, waiting for the right time to be revealed? This would change the entire world if it were true. I wanted to ask someone these questions. I knew the closest I would come to finding the answers was to ask the man who recognized my heart, my beloved priest.

I called him, and soon we were having lunch at his favorite restaurant. That's when I dared to ask the question, "Father, do you believe it is possible for a human to fully embody the divinity — to ascend?"

He smiled at me. He was all too familiar with my deep questions. He had been my priest since I was twelve, but this was the biggest question I had ever thought to ask. "Why do you ask?" He wasn't avoiding the question but rather pushing me to understand where I was taking this conversation.

"Scattered throughout different readings here and there," I explained, "I often think we only see glimpses of truth, teachings in which Christ was trying to tell us that we are just like him, that we are the physical embodiment of God. I think he was telling us that it's possible to live in heaven here on Earth. That, of course, I believe is also mixed in with other ideas that I see as nonsense, misinterpretation, or outright lies of those who wrote, rewrote, interpreted, or misinterpreted the Bible, in addition to the information that was lost while in translation of the original writings." I paused and smiled as I watched his eyes look hopelessly at me. I continued anyway, "But I think the truth is, this is the Second Coming, and it is within each of us, not one individual — that each one of us will one day realize who we truly are and will ascend not as spirit but as physical, human divine beings."

My priest looked at me. "I don't know, Kimberly. In seminary school, they were more interested in teaching us how to teach the Bible than how to contemplate topics like that. I think the meaning of life is to find joy in everything you do, and Christ is certainly the path to doing that. But whether any of us will truly experience the trinity of which you are talking about seems very unlikely in this life."

I was ready for that response, so I went further, "Father, I believe it has been done before. I believe the stories of divine and human mating. The Greek and

Roman mythology tales could be real, and those who suffered trying to live as divine beings in physical bodies did indeed exist, just as the divine mating of Mary and the Holy Spirit was real, resulting in Jesus living as both a god and a human."

"I suppose there is truth somewhere that we don't recognize hidden within the parables, in the Bible, or elsewhere. I have seen miracles, so I guess anything is possible." With his answer, I knew the conversation was closed with my questions still unanswered.

God and the Universe give us the gift of answers when we seek them. Often, when we believe there are no answers to the questions we seek, we are being shown a different path to eventually find our answers where we were not looking. The next morning, the Universe spoke to me through Mike Dooley, inviting me to a conference to become a certified Infinite Possibilities trainer.

Mike Dooley is the author of *Notes from the Universe*. His daily messages are full of reminders of how magical life is meant to be. Mike studied Abraham-Hicks, as I had years before, and he was a well-known expert in the law of attraction. He gained worldwide recognition through his appearance in the movie *The Secret* and his *New York Times* best-selling book, *Infinite Possibilities: The Art of Living Your Dreams*.

Although going to a conference to learn how to teach Infinite Possibilities was never on my radar, I recognized this was the Universe speaking to me. I knew that often we learn more when we teach rather than when we are students. Perhaps it was time for me to share so much of what I had learned — that we are responsible for the lives we create. So I took action and sent in my application for a scholarship to attend the Orlando conference in June of 2012, knowing in my heart that I would be accepted. Within a few days, I received my acknowledgment letter and the arrangements were in place. Somehow I knew I was meant to be there, and I knew my twin flame was close.

CHAPTER SIX

STANDING BEFORE YOU

A quickening of circumstances comes from an awareness that you are on a trajectory of a collision. The collision, of course, is that which you have created through your intentions, thoughts, emotions, and actions.

The morning before I left for the conference to become a trainer of Infinite Possibilities, I awoke to my beloved twin's voice. He told me it was time to write. When I first began working with my teacher, Bri, she told me a being on the other side wanted an audience with me. Unsure of exactly what that meant, I welcomed whoever wished to show up. As it turned out, it was the Archangel Gabriel who told me I would write — volumes — and that I would know in which order to bring the information to the masses. Although I appreciated the contact, I pretty much told Gabriel he had the wrong gal. Writing had never been my forte. I am dyslexic and I had nothing of importance to say to the world.

Awakening to my twin's promptings that it was time to write reminded me of the evening Gabriel first spoke to me. Was the meeting of my twin flame what Gabriel had wanted me to write about? I knew I was about to meet him — my twin. Images had been filling my head for days. Detailed snapshots of ordinary things seemed to jump out at me as if they were breadcrumbs leading me down a path. The cardinals that had spent the majority of their time alone now were a pair. They found great joy in tapping on my window and making their presence known. Something was about to happen, and the welcoming I felt to whatever it turned out to be removed any trepidation of attending a conference of this nature.

Infinite Possibilities is a program that principally teaches about the law of attraction. As I sat through each lesson, I concluded that the energy from the conference — the high so many people get from sessions and conversations with inspiring people — would assist me in working my energy into alignment with my purpose and joy. This I knew was one of the necessary ingredients to manifesting anything, and it would help bring my deepest desire to fruition: finding my twin.

From the moment I arrived at the hotel in Orlando, I felt a shift in my energy to pure centeredness. I met so many wonderful, open people. Having attended hundreds of professional conferences filled with egos and posturing at every turn, this environment felt surreal. I had never been with so many like-minded people, so many normal people. Yet I stayed on the fringe, engaging with people but still feeling more like an observer. As is typical in conferences of a spiritual nature, the audience was primarily female. The men I met were wonderful and engaging but certainly none of them was the twin I had come to know so well.

I did not expect him to be wearing a sign saying, "Hey, I'm your twin. I have come through eternity to find you" or that he was even necessarily going to be in attendance, but somehow the lack of his obvious presence disappointed me.

Awakening on Sunday morning, I felt the usual anxiety of the last morning of a conference. This stress usually comes when I need to be in a seminar and packed and out of the room at the same time. However, there was something else I was feeling too. I realized it was the thought of returning home to my life where people don't randomly hug each other "just because," where conversations are about the mundane details of life and not about life's magic. I felt the angst of being alone once again build the desire to find my twin flame. Through the realization of this feeling, I lost a bit of the peace of mind I had gained over the past few days.

Checking out between the last session and our final farewell lunch, I ended up in a long line listening to the ridiculous behavior of a guest checking in. Life was already returning to normal. As the guest's argument went on, my impatience for this woman rose and my impression of a very skilled desk manager grew. Watching her handle a very difficult situation with such kindness and grace and knowing I was missing the final lunch, I decided that it was more important to make sure kindness was recognized. After all, that was what we all wished for. As she assisted me to check out and apologized for the delay, I asked if I could speak to her supervisor. When he arrived, I told him in a voice loud enough for the desk manager to hear me, "Having been in hospitality and tourism for twenty-five years, I know your staff member deserves recognition for her outstanding ability to handle a challenging situation, and I wanted to personally tell you how impressed and appreciative I am of her abilities." With that out of the way, I shook his hand, winked at her, and walked on a cloud to the pool to join the others for lunch.

I found nearly everyone departing and giving final farewell hugs as they left to catch planes or to get on the road, excited to spread the message of Infinite Possibilities and thoughts becoming things. Feeling their love and the joy made me happy and grateful as I found my way to the buffet to fill my plate and enjoy the sun by the pool. My mood had shifted from the morning's feeling of loss to that of peace, even though I knew I had a four-hour drive ahead of me and an evening filled with family and mom responsibilities.

Turning to find a spot to sit, I suddenly saw a man standing before a table full of yummy treats and desserts. The childish grin he flashed at me made me catch my breath. Where had he come from? I had no idea, but looking at him, I knew at that moment I was a master manifester. I knew I created this moment of pure pleasure with everything I had. I could feel a connection so intense that the world around me disappeared, and I was one with All There Is again. I did not recognize him; I hadn't seen him all weekend. How could I not have seen him that entire time? The conference only had about 125 people in attendance. For a split moment, eternity froze in time, and I knew it was him — my twin flame.

My whole body was tingling with appreciation. He was physically everything I dreamed about. Tall, broad shouldered, and muscular with dark hair that hinted it would become curly if it were left long. His eyes were sapphire blue with the intensity of having lived many lifetimes. They were not crazy intense; they were safe and reassuring. Feeling my heart pounding in my chest and the weight of the plate still in my hand, I came back to the reality of here and now. And I smiled. Amused with myself for losing my sense of happiness and hope of finding him at the conference, I reached out my hand to introduce myself. On his right hand that met and embraced mine was the claddagh ring I had expected to see. Transcending from human to divine, I relaxed and enjoyed the surprise of his Irish brogue. He indeed was the man I had created; his ring was like Jamie's from *The Outlander*, but his heritage was not Scottish. It was Irish, and his dialect told me he was from somewhere near where my beloved priest had been raised. Lost in the soothing sound of his voice, I missed what he was saying completely as I stood in the awe of the moment. The emotional bliss of the connection needed no words.

Sitting together in the warm Florida sun while I began to eat, he asked me what I would be doing one year from this moment. My mind wondered if I should tell him the truth. Should I manifest that moment into existence like I manifested him? I was sure he was the twin flame I called forth. I knew I intended to be living with him in Ireland, but I held back what my heart wanted to say. Instead, I said with a bit of a cocky attitude, "I will be standing onstage telling the next group of new trainers how I met you today." With that, we both laughed.

He told me that he arrived in the States only a day before the conference began and on a whim made the trip to Orlando to attend. He wanted to take Infinite Possibilities and work with the youth in Ireland. He heard Mike Dooley speak in England many years before, and he knew Infinite Possibilities would bring change and hope to others as it had to him.

His heart belonged to a country that suffered for many generations. The youth in Ireland were depleted with the lack of work and hope. Many like him had moved to England in hope of finding work. A century and a half earlier, my own family had left Ireland in hopes of finding work and a new life.

Checking the time on my phone, I realized that minutes had turned into an entire hour. I gave myself permission to let go of my scheduled departure time and enjoy the present moment. His heart and passion inspired me, and I was swept up in his desire to help humanity heal from such long-held pain.

Twin flames' work is to assist humanity. The twins must each travel through their own personal journeys to achieve the wisdom needed to embrace their purpose. I wondered whether I had achieved this the way he seemed to. In my wonder, I searched his eyes for some clue, some knowing, to tell me that I had learned what I needed to help humanity.

Instead of finding my knowing, I found the eyes — the ones I was looking for that had been revealed to me in the vision of my twin flame. The sun perfectly aligned to ignite their color, and my heart stopped. It *was* him. He was my twin. His eyes showed me more confirmation. I knew then in that moment I was ready to live a life of purpose and meaning.

I knew nothing about this man, yet as we talked, I knew everything about him. I could somehow see all of him, his insecurities, his strengths, his longing, his brilliance, his desires, and his heart. I knew he could see me — all of me. With those eyes, he could see the place in my soul that I didn't even know existed. With no effort and no particular words, he made the space for me to feel safe and at home at last.

"I love your eyes. I have seen them a thousand times before." The words tumbled out of my mouth before I could stop myself. He looked back at me, astonished. I realized I didn't even know his name. I had missed it completely when he introduced himself. I was lost in the amazement of finding him.

"You have?" he said softly, seeming to know. He too felt the familiarity between us. We were lost in each other's eyes, and the silence between us allowed a communication to take place that spoke more than words ever could have. There was no awkwardness, just comfort and pleasure in the sun's warmth and each other's physical presence.

The attraction was not a familiar one for me. It was like a feeling of breathing again, being able to finally take a big, deep breath of air after enduring something stressful. I felt the sting of tears burning in my eyes more than once as the recognition of him reached my awareness on different levels. It was the sensation of needing to release everything I had been through in my life, as if I were someone who remained calm through a crisis, suddenly letting go of the bottled-up fear and knowing the worst was over.

We talked freely with each other, knowing that in any other company the thoughts we shared would have been ridiculed and judged as outlandish and crazy. The ease connected me further and deeper to my beloved, that twin I knew so well — yet so little about.

Soccer was a sport we were both passionate about, so we wandered to the bar to get out of the afternoon sun and catch the end of the Irish National team who was losing their bid for the World Cup soccer game. Knowing my sons were at home watching the game as well, I was sad that I had to tell him that I needed to leave, that I was expected at home. As the words came out of my mouth, I worked to steady my expression, not wanting him to realize how painful the thought was for me.

However, it was he who revealed himself and his anxiety at the thought of the separation. "Do you have to go now?" he asked. "Please stay. Please stay and have dinner with me." His eyes were desperate, begging me to say yes.

I couldn't find the words to say no. I could not force myself to leave him either, at least not yet. Excusing myself, I made a quick call home to my father, testing the waters of his reaction to me returning home late to my life.

"Hi! How did the conference go? Did you learn anything?" He seemed very happy to hear my voice, which gave me the sense that perhaps I needed to return sooner than I wanted to.

"Yeah, it was great, Dad. It really was. Ah, well, it was better than great. I met a really handsome Irishman, and I want to stay for dinner. Are you okay with that?" I cringed as those words came out of my mouth rather than giving him some sensible reason as to why I was already late, one that at least did not include a man. "It might be really late. I haven't left yet," I said, hoping he wasn't disappointed that I wasn't already on the road.

I realized my mind and heart were not working together, and at the moment, my heart was in charge. I knew that, yes, I was being irresponsible, but I wanted nothing more than to indulge myself, to be me — all of me — for just a little longer. An enthusiastic "Sure! You're not getting any younger!" from my father reached the comprehension part of my brain where the mixture of insult and permission slowly sorted itself out.

I let go of the insult part of the statement and said, "Thanks, Dad. Love you. Bye."

Now the only thing that stood between me and this man was my own fear. I sat and watched him for a few minutes, trying to decide between the unknown possibilities and the past that had crippled me for so long. Could all of this really be coming true? Could everything I wished for with every cell of my being truly be sitting and waiting for me? Was this day an illusion? Had I lost my mind and believed it was real? The sting of sunburn on my cheeks reminded me that it was real, and I was with the man I created from my pure desire. I wanted to believe it. I wanted to believe that fairy tales did have happy endings and that I could sail off with a partner just as Julia Roberts's character did in *Eat, Pray, Love.*

There was a time when I was in love with a boy, and rather than hear the answer to the double-dare question, "Do you love Kimberly?" I ran away as fast as I could, terrified that if I didn't, I would hear the word "no" — or something worse. I lived most of my life preferring not to know, instead believing that living alone was easier than suffering with a knowing that could break my heart.

The only way I was going to find out this time was to face my fears and trust that he would protect my heart, as I knew my twin flame would instinctively do. I got up, walked toward him, and began a long evening of connection that I had never before experienced in my life.

Over dinner in the quietest corner of the restaurant, we sipped wine, as people often do when there is recognition between them that there could be something more, we began revealing our secrets and our truths of how we had come to understand the world.

Laughing and storytelling, we each gave pieces of our soft parts away, watching the other for a reaction. One or two people left from the conference recognized us and stopped over to say hello. They seemed aware something was going on between us and would smile, hug us, and quickly leave. As the last person called him by name and he waved goodbye, I learned his name was Michael — like the archangel.

When it began raining, we decided to go to his room to continue our conversation. Now alone, our awareness of the intensity of the attraction between us became obvious. Yet we seemed to enjoy the control we both respectfully maintained. With each tale told of dyslexia struggles, being lost and alone while in our relationships, and the judgments we faced from the outside world, the reflection of ourselves in each other became clearer and clearer.

Feeling each experience with him as if living it myself, I felt my heart opening to witness who he was. Every deep laugh, every brush of his skin against mine, electrified every sense I had. Sitting on the dresser in his hotel room and watching him animate a crazy family story from his adventurous youth in Ireland, I received the one piece of information that confirmed without any doubt that Michael was my beloved twin flame. He was a twenty-first-century smuggler. I did it! I called in the One! And he was now standing before me. He was physical, his voice was no longer only in my mind, and he was real. How crazy is that? He was my needle in a haystack, and I called him forth.

Knowing I could be lost forever with this man, I decided it was time to pull myself away. Standing before me, in front of the elevator doors, was the man who would shift my reality forever. Waiting for the doors to open, he could no longer hold himself back from me. In one step, he traversed the distance between us, swept me up into his arms, and kissed me. I felt his breath fill my lungs as he whispered, "Stay with me." I wasn't sure whether I was even shaking my head no or not when he asked me for a good reason why I wouldn't stay the night with him. There was only one real answer, and I never told him.

In my heart, I wanted that day to remain forever perfect. I wanted his lips on mine and to hold that moment in my heart forever. In my mind, I wanted to keep every detail of the day exactly perfect the way it was. I wanted the anticipation of seeing him again to drive me wild. I wanted more wonder, more wanting him. I wanted to savor each moment of the revealing of who he was and who we could be together. I wanted the mystery. I wasn't running away; I was savoring the essence of my archangel.

"Michael," I whispered into his ear as the elevator doors opened, saving me from changing my mind, "if I stay with you, I will tarnish my halo, and we don't want that now, do we?" I said with a giggle, pulling him into the elevator with me and letting him kiss me again. I felt him absorb all of me in the moment we had left. As he pushed me against the elevator door, I could feel him asking for me. I could taste his sweetness, sharing his breath. I was lost in the intoxication of this man and his needing to know that I too was real.

• • •

Driving away from the man I spent my entire life seeking, I felt a new paradigm take hold. Somehow, I felt more myself, more whole and perfect. I felt as though my soul was recognized for the first time in my life. This feeling was not only from him witnessing and recognizing me but from me doing the same with my own eyes and all my senses. It was as if I was looking into a mirror and seeing someone I had once known. And as I remembered my love for him from another distant experience, I fell in love with my own reflection.

The parts of myself I always carried as crutches and weaknesses, we both shared. I accepted these things as part of what made Michael unique and beautiful, and through the mirrored reflection, they were now the things I could also love about myself. I recognized another odd feeling: I had an overwhelming sense that I was leaving home rather than going home. I felt overwhelmed by the sensation that he was sending me off to work or something, and when I was done, I would get to go home to him again. I was also aware of what I wasn't feeling. I was not feeling that short-breathed excitement when meeting someone I was interested in for the first time. Instead, I felt at peace, calm, collected, and awake. Awake like I had never been awake before.

As I pondered the absence of the expected excitement that I would have normally felt for a tall, handsome, charming man with a sexy accent, I became aware that it was not him. I was feeling the overwhelming love and excitement for myself. It was as if I could feel and love all of me through his eyes. I could feel a strong connection to him as a divine, living facet of God. I knew that I did not think or feel as I would have in the past — desperate to have him — because I already had him. We existed as one on some plane, dimension, or reality. I knew we were already together.

Driving through the dark night, I felt the light of the stars soaking into my skin. I was at peace not knowing whether I would ever see Michael again. I pulled my Moleskine notebook out of my purse and read his name, Michael Donnelly, tracing his handwriting with my finger. "Will I ever see you again?" I asked him, knowing he was asking the same question of me. He had written his phone numbers for England and Ireland and his temporary U.S. number next to his name. I smiled. Nice to meet you, Mr. Donnelly, after all this time.

I flipped through my phone to see the photo we took together. We looked as if we belonged together. I felt appreciative for the experience that most people will never know. I manifested my twin. I laughed out loud, knowing that I had so accurately created him, inspired by a man from a distant shore, long ago. I wondered if any other pieces of the Outlander story would manifest.

CHAPTER SEVEN

WAS IT ONLY A DREAM?

Is it possible to want something so badly that your mind rewrites reality? Words that are spoken have many meanings. Feelings that are expressed can be only a reflection of your own desire. Each of us experiences life through our own lenses of attitude, beliefs, and experience. Often the truth is only a mirror of our reflections.

As any twenty-first-century girl would do when floating on the high after a spiritual conference and meeting the man of her dreams, I woke up the next day and Googled Michael. I was relieved to find that he actually existed and his fanciful tales seemed to be true. I decided to wait a day before I sent him a text message: "Hope you're safely back in NY." He instantly replied with a photo of himself in a hardhat, posed at the construction site where he would be working over the next few months. Looking at the picture, I realized I knew exactly where he was. I had stood in that very place and taken a picture of the building across the street. The façade of the building was crowned with twin roses. It was a quiet street by New York's standards, not one someone would just happen by. The synchronicity of him standing in the same place where I once stood astonished me. I realized in that moment that this amazing love between us was really happening, and I could not quite shake the wonder of it all.

Over the next several weeks, we exchanged text messages and shared a few long conversations on the phone. For his birthday, I sent him some of my special homemade baked treats, which thrilled him. I basked in the enjoyment of having a man in my life again, even if it was long distance.

Late one night, my youngest son saw a text message come in on my phone from Michael that said, "Are you still up, Baby Face?" My new nickname amused both him and his brother into goofy hysterics every time my phone buzzed and Michael's picture flashed on the screen. But I liked it. I liked that my sons seemed to be at ease with my happiness. I enjoyed the intensified sensations that only exist when we are in love. And I liked the desire that thundered through me every time I heard his voice. It had been ages since I felt these feelings, the wanting of a man.

My creativity was spontaneous and my energy was abundant, even without sleeping. I busied myself setting up Infinite Possibilities training programs and classes. I was thrilled to share the information I learned at the conference with others.

I casually invited Michael to Florida several times without getting any confirmation of interest from him. I resigned myself to leaving it in the hands of the Universe to decide if I would ever see him again. It did not matter, because I was existing in the moment, loving my life and basking in my emotions while knowing all was well.

I shared with a girlfriend the romantic details surrounding my first meeting with Michael, and updates on conversations left us giggling like schoolgirls. She was an avid romance novel reader, so she found it especially enchanting. She made me vow to one day write a book about meeting a tall, handsome stranger from Ireland.

The memory of the touch of Michael's hand on my face and the gentle brush of a kiss he placed on my lips in his room still lingered alive. The promise of something much deeper that he showed me in the elevator, when he stared into my eyes and kissed me again, weakened me at the knees every time I let my mind wander back to that moment. There was a hunger that echoed through eternity awakening my soul once again.

Despite the joy I was feeling within my little world of spiritual enlightenment and connection with Michael, I would still run into the contrast that reality can provide. I often found my peace challenged while living in this very earthly life with its inhabitants.

Angry, aggressive, and rude people still crossed my path, despite the joy I was beaming into the world. Although I knew that handling these situations in a gentle, loving way was a gateway for me to gain a deeper understanding of relationships that I sought, it frustrated me. A happy girl can only take so much crap before she loses it, and it was on one of these days when I finally sent Michael this text message: "What I wouldn't give to spend another day with an enlightened soul like you." I am not sure what I intended the text to convey, but I felt good knowing he would understand what I meant by it.

What I did not expect was his reply: "Just come."

I stared at the message. What was he saying? Was this an invitation? Of course it was. How could I just show up in New York to meet with a man I barely knew? A string of possibilities raced through my head.

My mother's voice quickly jumped in. "But he could be a mass murderer." True, I thought, but I eliminated that possibility immediately.

"What if he turns out to be just a normal guy and all my dreams of finding my beloved twin come crashing down?" This seemed to be a strong possibility. And then I felt him. I felt the security and protection of his energy. I knew all would be well, no matter what happened. Besides that, I had been to the city many times, and I was very comfortable traveling there.

I replied, "I just might ;)" — not fully committing and giving him an out if I misinterpreted his offer.

His response was, "I'll pay for your ticket, just get here."

Okay, that definitely can't be misinterpreted as anything other than an invitation. Now it was up to me. What would I do? With that, I embarked on the uncertainty of the typical male/female relationship dynamic.

It took me just over twenty-four hours to decide I was going to visit him in New York City. Why not? I felt safe with him. I was an adult and had the time to go. How could I not go to see whether what I was thinking and feeling was really there? It was done, or at least I was done convincing myself. I let go and gave myself permission to go on this crazy, spellbinding adventure. I did all the research on flights, days, and times and sent him an email with all of the choices, and ... nothing. No response. I didn't even get a phone call or a text message from him that night.

My mind raced with questions. What did this mean? Did he think I wouldn't take him up on the offer? After three days passed with no word from him, my anxiety began growing, and every fear from every dark corner of my soul screamed at me. How could I have thought this too-good-to-be-true fairytale was real? I realized I needed to get a grip on my mind and emotions, but getting that foothold again was challenging with all my mental demons swirling around me.

"Breathe. Just breathe, Kimberly. That's all you have to do, and all will be exactly as it is meant to be. Trust in the Universe. You know this," I told myself over and over.

Yes, I did know this, and I already knew that in some reality we were together.

Aligning my vibration to that idea allowed me to relax into ease and grace again. Releasing my fear and panic, I let the Universe take over. Michael finally called me later that night.

"Hi, Baby Face," he said. "I hope your day was on top of the world. I'm sorry I haven't been able to call in a few days. I dropped my phone and just got it replaced this evening." I rolled my eyes, knowing that I had tortured myself for absolutely no reason, and took in the marvelous sound of Michael's brogue.

"I'm great. I'm on top of the world. Well, now I am," I chirped back, feeling like a ridiculous teenager. We resumed our usual conversation about my projects and progress and how his day had gone. Our conversations were usually about the things we were noticing around us and thinking about and feeling throughout the day. What I did not bring up with him was the email I sent him about the trip. I was going to leave it alone and see where it went.

Another week went by, and his mother and two sisters were due to come to the U.S. for a few days to attend a family wedding. As he shared the plans he had for them, it suddenly dawned on him to ask about my trip to New York. "Now, when are you planning on coming?" he asked, acting as if everything were already arranged. "My mother and sisters will be here for the week, and I want them to meet you."

What? Did I hear that right? He wanted me to meet his family? He might have mentioned that earlier, like when I sent the email that he never responded to. I knew he had been eagerly looking forward to seeing them, but I was *not* ready to meet any of his family yet, especially because he dearly enjoyed his sisters, one of whom was the center of his heart due to her simplicity and pure spirit of happiness. The other — an enthusiastic, fun-filled, rock-star spirit — traveled often with a professional Irish athletic team. I also knew he considered his mother to be his best friend, something I loved very much about him.

However, I did not necessarily think they would embrace some strange woman from Florida flying in to crowd their time with their beloved brother and son. I did not think this was a great way to start a new relationship in addition to the fact that I was a bit intimidated by his mother.

Having two sons of my own and being so close to them, I loved listening to Michael tell of the things he and his mother would do together. He respected her deeply. He seemed to really see who she was and what she had given up for his father and their family.

His parents met in Ireland when they were young, but a few weeks later, his father had an unexpected opportunity to travel to the United States, sponsored by his great uncle who lived in America. He left behind Michael's mother. Michael told me when she was young she was a bit of a spitfire and, after his father left her behind, she decided that she too would leave Ireland. She joined her sisters living in Canada. However, shortly thereafter, her sisters decided that she was a bit of a handful and took her back home to Ireland. Not to be dissuaded in her adventure, she decided to go to America to become a nanny and hopefully find her lost beloved. Of course, brave and determined girl that she was, she did finally find her man. And as the fairytale should go, she married him. Their children were born in Brooklyn, New York. When Michael was only six, they moved home to Ireland and opened a tavern. This was one fearless woman whom I admired, and I wondered whether I was following in her footsteps.

"Aw, Michael, I didn't make any airline reservations, so I don't have plans to come see you. I am sorry. I sent you an email, but you never responded to it, so I kind of assumed that it would not work for you," I stammered, feeling a bit awkward.

"Kimberly, I didn't see the email. Please tell me that you won't ever worry if you haven't heard from me. Just know that everything is okay, all right?" He said this with such sincerity that it removed the need to ever worry about stupid male/female insecurities again.

He looked up my email, and we made plans for me to visit the weekend after his family left. I booked the flight with no discussion about accommodations, feeling once again the ease of allowing myself to flow into alignment with my dreams, and trusting, as he asked, that everything was okay.

CHAPTER EIGHT

TESTING A NEW REALITY

> *"Our deepest fear is not that we are inadequate. Our deepest fear is that we are powerful beyond measure."*
>
> — *Marianne Williamson*

My plane was sitting on the runway waiting for our turn to take off as the captain's voice came over the intercom: "Sorry, folks. We were hoping to take off before Air Force One was scheduled to arrive, but they have shut down the runway a few minutes early. We will take off as soon as possible. Sit tight."

The delay wasn't much of a surprise; I was traveling during mercury retrograde (travel and communications typically go askew during this astrological aspect). I turned my phone back on and posted to Facebook that I was delayed waiting for President Obama to make his landing in Southwest Florida. At least I would have a front row seat.

My Republican friends jumped at the opportunity to make unfriendly comments and snipes about their least favorite president, filling my Facebook feed instantly. Not wanting to engage in the drama, I closed my eyes and revisited my plan as it was. Actually, I had no plans other than arriving at JFK and making my way into the city to meet Michael at work.

I'd visualized the scene a thousand times already: me sashaying up the street, locking eyes with him, and feeling my heart pounding in my chest as I fell into his thick, strong arms. He would catch me and kiss me, hailing catcalls and whistles from the workers up and down the street.

He was working for the construction company of an old friend, Leland, who was undergoing cancer treatment. Michael was also living in Brooklyn with Leland and his family. I did not know where we were going to stay while I was in town. I wasn't sure whether he made arrangements for me or I would be sleeping on the street, but at least I would be with him. And that was enough of a promise to risk the unknown.

I did have a backup plan, just in case. I called a few friends in the area, letting them know I would be in town on a pure faith adventure meeting a tall, handsome Irishman whom I had only seen once before. That idea did not seem to bother any of my friends at all; each one assured me that I would have a great time and congratulated me on finally meeting someone who had stolen my heart. It gave me a little bit of stability knowing they would be there in a flash if I needed them.

My male friends at home assured me that Michael would take care of the accommodations even though we didn't discuss it. They explained it is the man's responsibility to arrange for lodging as part of the invitation, but it was making me a bit nuts. I vacillated daily between trust and "this is insanity" thoughts. Normally I am the one responsible for making all the plans, but this time, everything was different. I was going to allow myself to be taken care of, a new concept for me. I reached into my carry-on bag, once again verifying my backup hotel information was there in the event that I did need a place to stay. And because blindly following my bliss was new to me, I called the hotel the night before to check their projected availability. The thought of Elizabeth Gilbert in Bali flashed through my mind one more time as I watched Air Force One touch down on the runway, and I smiled. Well, here we go into the beyond.

• • •

Exiting the Jet Blue terminal, I looked down at my phone, and my stomach dropped. My phone's battery only had 30 percent power left. That would never do going into the city to meet Michael. I resisted the urge to just wing it and found a place in the airport to plug my phone in and let it charge while I got myself a snack. In New York, it's normal for things to either happen really fast or take forever. In the past, I always jumped on the train and made it to the city within thirty minutes. Today, it was going to take forever.

My phone took a long time to charge, but it was enough to get me through the afternoon on roaming. A friendly man sitting next to me talked me into taking the bus into the city. The bus may have been as easy and cheap as he promised, but he neglected to mention the time it took for it to leave the airport and stop at every single terminal on the way out, which seemed like forever. To top it all off, it was pouring rain.

Just after the bus left the airport, Michael called to tell me he was leaving work early so that he could he pick me up. I informed him I was already on the way, so we agreed to meet in front of Grand Central Station instead. My vision of meeting Michael on the Upper West Side, the sun illuminating my hair as I ran into his arms, was now completely gone, and I began to worry whether this weekend was going to work out at all.

Once in Manhattan, I stood across the street from the station to stay out of the rain. I passed the time by reviewing in my mind how crazy I must be to be standing in New York waiting for a man. I considered how I hadn't dated anyone in years. I still had lingering fears and issues about men from my marriage. I also had very little time for a relationship in my life, yet here I stood, waiting like I had nothing else better in the world to do. I looked down at my phone and began to feel panic arise as I watched the bars disappearing. And then I heard his voice. "Kimberly."

Looking up, I saw him across the street smiling and waving at me. Barely glancing at traffic, I dashed through the raindrops and honking horns into his arms, tasting his lips on mine once again. He took my breath away, and the raindrops washed away all my fears. I was in bliss.

As we drove off into city traffic, I resisted the urge to ask where we were going. Almost as if he read my mind, he reached over and took my hand. "I borrowed Leland's bungalow for the weekend. It's small and quaint. It's been in his family since it was built in the thirties. We have had a lot of good times there over the years. Have you been to Rockaway before?"

"No, I haven't," I said, charmed by his choice of accommodations. "I have only stayed in Manhattan." I recalled a friend who rented a house on the beach while she was in medical residency. She loved it there. She spoke often about the dunes and the seabirds that migrated through the area. I blushed at the thought of Michael choosing such a romantic location.

Later that evening, after I settled into the guest bedroom that Michael prepared for me, we sat outside on the bungalow's steps. Sitting together with our shoulders touching, we watched the sun disappear while the last of the day's beachgoers gathered their things to leave. I could feel the strength of his body and the ripples of his muscles. A month and a half of physical labor had toned him into the masterpiece of Irish legends. I knew it took him awhile to get used to the physical nature of the work. He hadn't worked in construction since he was in his early twenties, but he was pleased to be in action again, at least for a few months.

Michael had only made a few plans before I arrived, so he asked me what I would like to do while I was visiting. The list scrolled through my head like a well-worn reel. I thought, "Well, I would like to know whether I have made up this fantasy of how wonderful you are. I want to see you around friends and family to find out if they think you are wonderful too. I would like to —" I looked up, realizing he was expecting a verbal answer of some kind and answered him with a simple truth. "All I planned to do is spend time with you and get to know you. I have visited New York many times in the past, so let's just do what comes." Michael paused and looked at me with those eyes that revealed his soul, and a huge grin stretched across his face, matching mine. It was settled. Our plan was to simply enjoy each other.

We walked a few blocks down the road to eat dinner at a restaurant that was a favorite of the locals. It had been many years since I was in a relationship with a man. I was aware of how our strides matched as we walked. Reaching out and taking my hand, Michael pulled me close to him, staying between the street and me. My mind noticed every detail of our interaction. I thought how strange all of this felt; it was so new and interesting.

I'm not short by any means, standing at just over 5'7", but he still made me feel tiny in comparison. He was not only tall and strong; it was more than that. He made me feel protected and cared for, almost as if I were a child. It was a good feeling, but one that I also felt resistance to. I was alone for many years, and letting myself suddenly become helpless was not a part of my plan.

Rockaway and the adjoining Grassy Point have long been a summer playground for those who live in Brooklyn. What was once a peninsula sprinkled with non-weatherized bungalows on postage stamp–sized lots is now a year-round community with modern homes replacing the old charm. Despite the transition over the years, everyone still seems to know each other. Michael and I were greeted at the restaurant as if we were old family.

I became aware that the majority of the accents I was hearing around me were Irish of varying degrees. It did not surprise me that the chatter revolved around a big Irish football game that was happening the next day. What did surprise me was that Irish football is not soccer nor is it American football. It is one of two unique sports played in Ireland, the second being hurling. Michael's father was well known in the area during his football years, both in New York and at home in Ireland. Michael also did well in the sport and was known by the locals for the days past when he lived and played as a young bachelor with his friend Leland.

I learned that Michael had a reputation for helping anyone who came to the

States from Ireland, for providing a place to stay and helping them find work. He was popular and well remembered for his wit and charm that extended well past sweeping only me off my feet.

Dinner was quite enjoyable. I was amused by Michael's modesty as his old friends stopped to greet us and boast about his fame. I was impressed that, despite the passing of more than twenty years, he was able to fall right back into the community again.

Walking back to the bungalow with my hand in his, he broke the silence of the night, squeezing it and apologizing that our night was less than private, as he hoped for. I leaned into him, wrapped my arms around his arm, and said, "Tonight told me exactly what I wanted to know about you."

"Oh yeah, what's that? That I was a dumb jock when I was a kid?" He laughed.

"No, that you are loved, and it's not just me who is crazy about you," I said softly, slowing looking into his eyes.

I have spent much of my life being a helper to the men I loved. Whatever they needed, I would retrieve and take care of it. It began when I was four years old when I was Cecile's helper at my grandfather's store. I sought not the attention of my father figure, as Freud suggests, but the first man I recognized who loved me. Cecile recognized my little bright soul, and for that I loved him. He was a man who would do anything for me and treasured spending time with me. Later, after my grandfather passed away, Cecile sent me a letter with a tiny photo of me. It was my kindergarten picture, and the caption read, "My little helper and sweetheart." It told me how much he cherished me after all those years.

Michael was looking at me with the same loving heart. However, Michael was not looking at me as if I was a little beloved child. His gaze held something deeper. This is how men, real men, look at the women they love. I felt ridiculous. My heart was racing, and my knees were quivering. I was willing him to sweep me up and take me to the bungalow and make love to me. Instead, he traced my face with his finger, taking in every detail, and gently kissed me on the forehead. His body leaning against mine gave him away too, assuring me I was not alone in my desire.

I was so busy trying to sort out my feelings for him — how could I feel this way for a complete stranger from across the Atlantic — that it never occurred to me how much he could like me. My relationships in the past were not with men like Michael. He was perhaps the first man I recognized as someone who just simply enjoyed me for me, laughing, sharing, and being present. I did not have to work for his attention; it was there naturally. In the restaurant, he never took his eyes off of me except to speak to someone. When he did, he would introduce me, and as soon as they left, he would fill me in on the background of who they were and the connection he had to them. He made me feel as if I were the center of his attention, something new and foreign to me.

At forty-four years old, I was well past pretending or playing games; however, the energy surging through my body was not matching my plan of remaining calm, cool, and collected. In fact, I had no intention of sleeping with him while I was in New York. I was interested in Michael as a man and not a playmate or a one-time lover.

I spend most of my time with my sons and their friends; couple that with the fact that I hadn't been in a relationship for several years, and I had nearly forgotten that I was a woman who at one point had a considerable sexual appetite. My focus was lost in getting to know Michael, so it never occurred to me how I would handle the raging sexual desire that was now coursing throughout my body. Somehow he took control and recognized that the little country girl in me who now walks around in four-inch heels like she belongs in this big, grown-up world was not "that" kind of girl, and he seemed to like it.

When we returned to the little bungalow, still preserved for the traditional use of a summertime family getaway, I found a beach blanket. Holding it up with a smile, he nodded, grabbed a bottle of wine, and led me outside. Despite the modern furnishings and upgrades to the kitchen, both the bedrooms were furnished with bunk beds to accommodate family and friends. I doubted we could both fit and sleep on a twin bed. Reassured that we both planned to preserve my integrity. I took a deep, salty breath and worked to center myself, feeling safe and happy.

Lying on the blanket under the stars, the waves crashing against the shore, I snuggled into Michael and relaxed as he talked about his family at home. His three sisters still lived in Ireland. They had each found good men, and he told me how happy and grateful he was for that. I was happy for them as well. In the comfort of his arms, I knew at long last I too had found a good man.

Later that night, we each retreated reluctantly to our own rooms and tried to sleep, tossing and turning, feeling the ridiculousness of the four-inch wall between us. Saturday morning came, and despite the lack of sleep, we got up early. Michael poured me some tea while I watched him make himself porridge. He offered me some of this traditional Irish breakfast, but I passed. It made me think back to the Outlander series. Jamie was a porridge man too; Claire, his wife, not so much. I giggled to myself at the similarity and my agreement.

My grandfather, who was my beloved hero, also ate porridge or oatmeal, but he was never able to convince me of its value to make the day a good one. His appetite for bread, crumb buns, apple pie, cream puffs, and similar traditional Irish treats I was all for, but never oatmeal. Michael seemed a bit concerned that I was not eating breakfast, the most important meal of the day. I assured him breakfast was not my forte. Finally giving in, he seemed satisfied that I would eat as soon as we got into the city.

Our plan for the day included visiting the former location of the World Trade Center. It was something both Michael and I wanted to see, but neither of us had gotten the opportunity to visit and pay our respects to those who passed away on that fateful day. Michael researched the disaster and didn't believe the "official" story of what happened that day, and I agreed the whole story had not yet been revealed to us. The only truth that was unarguable was the loss of 2,749 people who were in the prime of their lives forever changed the world. Visiting the site with Michael seemed like the perfect way to spend the morning. I knew he also grieved the loss of every one of those souls.

Michael told me our evening was planned so that we would have to return early. I wasn't sure what he had up his sleeve for that night, but he seemed pleased with himself and kept it a secret. He wanted to surprise me, and I was very happy. I packed a sexy black dress to wear — just in case something nice came up.

Walking to the subway was a far more daring feat than I had expected. Michael took my hand and guided me through the streets and passing cars that were coming in for the weekend. My eyes searched for the nearest crosswalk, but I quickly learned that jaywalking was normal for him. He had the intuitive ability to pull me into his body just as I was about to get creamed by a car or truck driver who also agreed we should be using the crosswalk.

Navigating the subway with him was the same as the street. I had been in the city countless times, and I was always counted on to be the tour guide, watching the subway stops so that I knew where we needed to get off. Michael may have considered himself a country Irishman, but he was a natural at city living. The years he spent in the States as a young man gave him confidence that I quickly learned to enjoy. However, not knowing this and expecting to be as in charge of myself (if not everyone else) as usual, I found it challenging to carry on our conversation and know where we were at each stop. As I became very confused and felt my anxiety creeping in, Michael intuitively held up three fingers and winked at me. Seeing in his eyes that he was in control and a little amused by my need to be in control, I began watching him instead of everything around me.

In that moment of giving over and trusting him, we connected like the final two pieces of a puzzle. It was done; we were now moving as one. In mid-sentence, his glance toward the subway doors told me our stop was next. After a screeching halt, we exited and emerged in lower Manhattan without interrupting our conversation.

Moving as one through the quiet weekend streets of the financial district, we found our way to Ground Zero. Michael, like so many others, had lost a family member on that tragic day. His cousin, a firefighter, lost his life when tower one collapsed. His cousin had the trademark family eyes. They could have been brothers; there was such a strong family resemblance.

Michael told me the night before that no one had ever mentioned anything remarkable about his eyes. He had his father's eyes. He told me that when he talked to his father, he felt power and comfort in his eyes, and he missed that very much. His modesty continually surprised me, and how he managed to live so many years without ever getting married surprised me even more.

We visited each side of the nearly completed monument telling the story of heroism and loss. It was quite moving, but instead of finding a sacred space filled with honor and respect, we were pushed and pulled by the crowd of people who were hoping to find the names of their loved ones. We retreated from the masses, deciding that perhaps it would be better if we moved out of the city itself and into the boroughs to find a bite to eat. Michael also wanted to peek in on the Irish football game that was going on that day. Finding our way into the Bronx to Leland's brother's Irish pub, we were finally able to relax from the intensity of the morning.

In a truly authentic Irish pub surrounded by rich Irish characters, I watched Michael interact in the traditional "I buy, you buy" drink rounds while cheering for his team. He stopped occasionally to test me to make sure I understood his explanation of the game. When I passed on all accounts — interaction, game rules, scoring, and the like — he beamed at me. He was at ease here, and he seemed happy that I enjoyed his favorite sport.

Not ever leaving my side, he whispered details about the people who were in the crowd around us. With every introduction, I recognized Michael's ability to connect the dots in almost every situation. Ireland was not that big of a country, and many people had moved from Ireland to New York at one time or another, creating a network of people who were either friends or family. I laughed as I thought to myself how virtually everyone I knew claimed to have Irish roots too. I wondered if Ireland was indeed the glue of six degrees of separation.

As Michael paid our bill, a young Irishman new to the country cajoled him into playing a round of pool. Apparently, at one time it was rumored that Michael was rather proficient at the game. With a glance at me and the clock, his eyes asked, "What do you think?" I nodded with the delight of a young girl about to receive a prize at the carnival, so he agreed to just one game.

With Michael now occupied and my propensity for being a magnet to old men wherever I went, I quickly befriended what I thought was a sweet old Irishman. I watched Michael break the balls with expert precision and a loud crack from across the room. During the game, much to my surprise, I found that not only was this old man *not* feeble but also a shark in both games — pool and women. Michael, who was completely unaware of my situation, studied the table and dropped the solids one by one into the pockets as this fresh old man tucked a piece of paper into my hand. Looking down at the scribble on the note, I saw his phone number. I shot Michael a dirty look for leaving me and tried to give the number back to my new suitor. Being a professional shark, he stood his ground undaunted while overtly winking at me. Rolling my eyes at this little man who barely stood five feet tall, I caught Michael's pained expression as his eight ball missed the pocket. Within minutes, the young Irishman took his opportunity and cleared the table of all stripes, pocketing the eight ball and his winnings with a fancy bank off the pool table wall. "Next time, call me when you are in town," the old man said with a nudge and another wink. Michael and I had both been put in our place.

As a perfect gentleman, Michael thanked the young man for the spanking and the old man for "providing me company" while he was playing and said his final goodbyes, leading me quickly in the direction of the door. Grateful to be leaving, I informed him of my new suitor. I firmly placed the old man's number into his hand, just in case he wanted to make a call someday. Not even slightly flustered or sympathetic, he let me spend the next twenty minutes pouting in my own drama. So much for my hero rescuing me. Not that I needed rescuing from a ninety-year-old man, but it would have been nice if Michael had at least put a teasing claim on me. He did, however, slip the number into his pocket with a raise of his eyebrow.

When we arrived back in Rockaway, the calm from the day before was gone, replaced with music, kids riding bikes, and loud families enjoying their day in the sun. With merely two feet between houses, there was a sense of togetherness that was inescapable. All of the neighbors had known Michael's and Leland's families for decades, and they were interested that he had, at last, brought a woman to the beach with him. With this bit of information, my mood immediately lightened. "So," I questioned the overly friendly woman next door, "Michael is not the player he could be?"

"Oh, no!" she exclaimed. "He is a shy, sweet boy. For years we wondered if he might be funny," she said with the flick of her hand. I laughed at the thought, and that she had actually said it. Seeing my expression, she continued, "No, no, he has always been too busy working and helping everybody out. He always fixes this or that, whatever anyone ever needs help with."

"Good afternoon, Mrs. MacCrain." Michael's voice came over my shoulder as he walked up and leaned his body against mine. He pushed his knee into the back of mine, unsteadying me and letting me know he knew exactly what I was up to. He reached around me and handed me a cup of hot tea, made to my exact liking. "I'm sorry to tear Kimberly away from you, but we have to get ready for the special night I have planned."

"Oh yes, I heard at the grocery that you were going on the cruise abound Manhattan. That is so nice, and it's romantic too," she said with a knowing smile. Michael groaned in the back of his throat as she revealed his secret plan.

I turned to face him, grinning from ear to ear. "Yes, indeed, that sounds romantic," I agreed, trying to contain my excitement in front of Mrs. MacCrain. I was amused with just how small this town seemed to be.

Shaking his head, Michael led me into the bungalow and asked if I was enjoying myself. "Quite so! And I am very glad you turned out to not be 'funny,'" I said with a flick of my hand.

"I will show you funny," he said in almost a whisper so that Mrs. MacCrain could not hear, pulling me into him and guiding me to the couch. He lowered me onto it with one swoop. My heart was pounding in my chest. As he kissed me all over, I melted into his intensity. My bliss was interrupted by his deep, serious voice against my ear. "And the next time a man gives you his number, I expect you to drop him. Did your father never teach you that?"

"No," is all I could say as he claimed my body. I let my head fall back with the power of his consumption and with the pleasure of him becoming my hero after all.

An hour later, my face now raw from his kisses, I stood in the shower with my hand against the wall to support my body, throbbing for want of him. His self-control stunned me. I was putty in his hands, but he refused to take me. Instead, he was teasing and romancing me. When he had realized his afternoon shadow had left my face burned, he left to find something that would soothe my skin. I got into the shower to get ready for our evening. If I had not heard from so many people that he was the man he was, I would have surely thought he was playing me. He did seem to know every note, chord, and vibration that turned me on. He was the man of my dreams, and each moment I spent with him made me weaker and stronger at the same time.

When he returned with the skin balm, he found me wrapped in just a towel, hair dripping down my back. For a split second, I recognized that he was not as in control and centered as he appeared to be. He stopped at the bathroom door and steadied himself against the frame. Reaching for another towel, he gently dried my shoulders. Secretly, I reveled in the moment. I taunted him with my eyes and a slight smile. His lips parted to say something, but he paused and smiled, closing his eyes and inhaling my freshly showered scent of lavender. When he opened them again, I stepped out of the bathroom, brushing my body lightly against his as I made my way to the bedroom.

Unsure if he was taunting me or just lacking modesty, I heard him strip and drop his clothes on the floor without closing the bathroom door. I couldn't resist glancing back over my shoulder to find him stepping into the shower, looking at me. His naked body took my breath away.

• • •

The yacht was stunning. I felt as if I had been taken away into a fairy tale as I boarded the ship arm in arm with my handsome prince. As amazing as he looked in a pair of jeans and a tight T-shirt that revealed his muscular frame, wearing a suit, he looked as if he belonged in the pages of *GQ*.

Leaving the port with champagne in hand, I wished I had brought a wrap to go with my little black dress. Michael saw the chill roll through my body and pulled me tight against him, intoxicating me with his scent. Breathing deeply, I traced the elegant design on his tie. "Do you like it?" he asked.

"Very much. You have impeccable taste," I said, smiling up at him.

"Thank you, but the credit has to go to my sister. She helped me pick it out when she was here last week."

"Oh, was this evening her idea too?" I thought I must thank her one day.

"No, this was all me and something I have always wanted to do, but I never had someone special to do it with. Leland just isn't the kind of company I like to keep on romantic evenings." He laughed.

Looking up into his eyes, I marveled at how much I had fallen in love with this man, knowing that not long ago I had decided that I never needed someone in my life to find happiness. I felt grateful that the Universe knew better.

I could lose myself completely while looking into his soul through the windows of his eyes. I was finally willing to let myself be in the awe of love. He traced the back of my hairline, wrapping his finger in the blowing tussles of hair that had fallen loose. "Do you have any idea how lovely you are, Kimberly?"

I didn't respond. I only breathed him in more, not looking away from his gaze.

"I have watched you since you arrived yesterday," he continued, "and I don't think you know how beautiful you are, how people turn to look as you walk by. I know now why I never got married. I knew there was a reason, and you were that reason."

Speechless, tears filled my eyes, and he took my face in both hands, searching to see what was wrong. "Joy!" I said, smiling at him and leaning forward to meet his kiss.

Michael had reserved a window table for two. We laughed and enjoyed the wonderful dinner and service as the sunset gave way to a twinkling Manhattan skyline. I got lost in his stories about his homeland; they both tickled and inspired me. Over the main course, he turned the tables on me. "I want to know what it has been like raising two sons on your own."

Raising my boys is something I've never felt challenged by. It's not only because they are great kids and easy but that I love being their mom. I feel honored almost every day to be a part of their lives. They are my world. I could see the admiration in Michael's eyes as he enjoyed his salmon and I, my filet mignon au poivre.

I realized he loved me as much for being a mother as for being a woman. In our daily conversations, he always asked about my boys. He remembered details from our day-to-day activities and always followed what they were doing. That was something I very much appreciated about him. It made me feel at ease being who I was with him. After our dessert, we went onto the deck to watch the night sky as we sailed under the Brooklyn Bridge.

Standing in silence, wrapped in the warmth of each other, we listened to the music coming from the lower deck until I could sense the seriousness within him. I could no longer ignore it. "Michael, what's wrong?" I asked.

"I have two very important questions I want to ask you, and I am afraid I may not like the answers you give me," he said in a slow, raspy voice.

Searching his face for what could possibly be on his mind during such an intimate moment, I said, "You can ask me anything."

Pausing, he took a deep breath. "Would you ever leave this place and move across the ocean? Do you think you could do that?" He nodded in the direction of Europe.

His question brought an awareness I had never felt before. I was bonded to him. For the first time in my life, I felt bound to someone, connected to him. I knew I would follow him anywhere to be by his side. I knew what true love was, but this was different. This was a bonding that felt beyond worldly. We were as one, one soul. Without words, I nodded, and he knew I would always be at his side. "Would you have a child with me?" he asked, nearly holding his breath.

"Only if we get to practice a lot!" I said, teasing him. He sighed and released all his fear. I raised my eyebrow as an invitation for the "dessert" I was hoping for later that night.

"Well, you do get better with practice, you know," he said, "and truthfully, I am a bit rusty." I was shocked, not believing he said that, and realized he was reflecting the same trepidation that I was feeling. We let go, relaxed, and spent the rest of the night playing on the dance floor.

Losing the boundaries between us as the night progressed, we shared a bottle of wine on the now quiet Rockaway shore. Wrapped up together in blankets, we opened our souls and shared secrets never told before. We were not afraid to ask each other anything nor to be shunned for our feelings and answers. Being with him was as natural as breathing. With each kiss, he brought forth a woman, leaving behind the girl and mother I had identified with for so long. His powerful physical male presence balanced my feminine softness that he had called forth. The now familiar sensation of being whole and witnessed by someone filled my senses. I was crazy about this man, and I knew I truly loved him.

Our bodies became closer, embracing what our souls were experiencing. I wanted to know him on all levels — mentally, emotionally, spiritually, and physically.

In the cover of clouds, I slipped my panties off and tucked them into his shirt pocket. He smiled at me, knowing that I was finally his. I slid on top of him, undoing his belt as he watched. With his manhood finally freed from its frustrating confines, we immersed ourselves in the pleasure only physical bodies can provide. We both moaned with the intensity of the bliss we were feeling. He grabbed my hips to keep me from moving. I struggled against him, wanting and needing to move. Our eyes locked, now motionless and breathless. He nodded, and I exploded in pure pleasure and bliss.

In one motion, I was on my back, and I disappeared from the reality of this world. He found a rhythm that matched the waves and my body's desire, sending me into the Universe to witness our soul's birth. I was the divine chalice of the feminine, and he was a masculine god filling me with divine love. Our bodies were alive with the frequency of light and love. I could feel the radiance of our union. I could feel our hearts beating together as one. I came over and over again in a dizzying, breathless surrender to love. When he finally came, I had nothing left to give him, my body shaking, feeling his power as he filled me with his essence. His eyes never left mine, watching as tears filled them and overflowed with my emotion. We were complete.

• • •

After soundly sleeping through the night on one of the many twin bunk beds, I awoke with the first dawn light streaming through the window. Hearing the neighbor giving instructions to her husband to go get some fresh pastries, I pulled on some yoga pants, twisted my hair in a knot, and headed for the deck.

My routine most mornings is spending time meditating and visualizing. But Rockaway is not Fort Myers, and finding peace and tranquility is not a part of borough life. After meeting the neighbor and several people passing by while sitting on the steps to the beach in an attempt to meditate, I finally gave up. I quietly found my shoes and wandered down the now familiar streets of the neighborhood.

Peering into windows of businesses and enjoying the cooler weather of the northern morning, I let my mind wander. I discovered a new sense of peace that was all its own. Reviewing all that I was learning about myself, I became aware of how ready I had become for a relationship. My mind sorted through my last relationship, and an appreciation grew from what I had once chalked up to disaster into a realization of how much healing had been created at that time.

Thinking of Michael's hand around my wrist as I passed his favorite jaywalking location, I remembered a time when I would not have let someone touch my wrists. Nor would I have let them put their hands on my shoulders as Michael did when he wrapped his arms around me. My historic response would have been to flinch and shake off that kind of touch. The years that I have spent alone and each relationship I've had, no matter how insignificant it was, healed me in some way from the abusive marriage I was once in. Each interaction, big and small, healed me and taught me that I could trust myself again.

Michael was the man I created on mornings much like this and nights spent reading about Jamie, a loving man who lived in another time and place. "He is a good man," the voice of my grandfather clearly said to me. I smiled. I often relied on his advice from beyond this world. He always wanted a good man for me. He wanted me to feel loved and happy. I remembered a poem he wrote for me to let me know that until the day someone stole my heart away, he would be there to let me know I would always be loved. The thought of him filled my eyes with happy tears. As I walked, a white feather drifted down to the sidewalk, assuring me that indeed it was his voice I had heard. He was with me, loving and guiding me. The feather was his signature that he was still with us.

Everyone in my family has experienced finding a feather just as they were thinking or speaking about my grandfather. He often watches over me, and I had very much felt his presence over the past few days. Bending to pick up the feather, I smiled, thinking about how protected and special he always made me feel. I missed that feeling dearly. I had nearly forgotten how good it felt until Michael reminded me once again. Dashing into a coffee shop, I picked out my grandfather's favorite pastries and a large coffee and headed back to Michael.

• • •

Riding the train on the way to Michael's aunt's house, I leaned against him and closed my eyes. I was happy that he'd asked me whether I minded visiting her. He hadn't seen her since his return from Ireland and thought she might like to meet me. Unaware of how strong my Irish genes were, I was welcomed in with open arms by this adorable, not-quite-five-feet-tall Irish saint, who was also "thrilled to meet an Irish girl." Franny had only met one girl from Michael's past relationships, whom she said was an "English snob," so I turned out to be a bit of a novelty. Feeling a bit bad about disappointing her, I provided her my list of genetic ancestry: Welch, Scottish, Slovak, and yes, Irish.

Undaunted about the mixed blood, Franny scooted into the kitchen to make us some refreshments and treats. Her apartment was tiny and charming. It reminded me of some of my relatives, now passed, who had lived in Connecticut. I always loved visiting their places, and no matter who I was visiting, I always felt right at home. Franny's place had that same familiarity.

Fran had once been a nun. It was not her choice but rather one of her family's pride. She left her order shortly after her father passed away. As we talked, I noticed the same sparkle in her eyes that Michael had. Watching her as she caught Michael up with what was happening in their family, and as she shared stories and pictures of his father with me, I felt as captivated with her as I was with Michael. I shared my photos of my boys and stories about their love of soccer and their Catholic high school — or rather the girls in the school. The time passed quickly with the ease of her grace.

Regretting leaving only a few hours after we arrived, we said our goodbyes and I promised I would visit the next time I was in town. I enjoyed watching Michael with his aunt. The closeness and the love they shared made me miss the days when my family was bigger with aunts, cousins, and my grandparents.

As Michael and I walked away, arm in arm, toward the subway on our way to visit Coney Island, I asked him if we could take Franny out to dinner the next time I visited. He answered me with a smile.

Coney Island was packed wall to wall with people. It took my breath away in an entirely different way than Michael did. Knowing I was leaving the next morning, I ignored the people-watching opportunity and instead savored the small details about Michael. I deliberately reviewed them in my mind, making sure I would remember them. Even though I had never been to Coney Island before, it felt very familiar. Nathan's Famous Coney Island Restaurant's annual hotdog eating contest was a must-watch at my house, so as we walked by the stand and read the names of the winners, I somehow felt like a part of the place already.

We found our way into the aquarium by weaving through the families that filled each room, enjoying the beauty of the sea life. Michael leaned over and said something to me. I nodded yes, but he knew I had not understood him. He stopped me and asked, "What do you call the thing you put a baby in and push them?" pointing to one of the many strollers that crowded the dark room.

"A stroller?" I said, confused.

"Yes, yes," he said. "We are lucky to have gotten in here without a pram. We call them prams in Ireland," he explained. The sudden realization that this man lived an ocean way from me came crashing into my reality, and I had to find my way out of the crowd and get some air.

Standing outside, I began digging through my purse looking for a cigarette. It was the first time I felt the desire to smoke all weekend. I looked up at him, shaking my head back and forth. "How long are you going to be in New York?" I asked unceremoniously.

Unsure whether I was upset about the baby comment or what he said about Ireland, he said strongly but in a calm demeanor, "Tell me what just happened in there."

"Michael, I am leaving in the morning, and I have no idea if or when I will ever see you again." I almost choked on the words, searching his eyes for answers.

"I don't have any plans, Kimberly, but so far it has been working out pretty well since I got here, so let's just believe everything will work out just like it is supposed to, okay?" Not particularly satisfied with his answer, I agreed anyway, and we found our way back to the boardwalk and eventually the train station.

• • •

As we worked together in the kitchen preparing the cheese, bread, and a bottle of wine we had picked up on the way home, I asked him if he had returned his mother's call from earlier in the day. He hadn't, which made me a bit crazy because my sons had also not called me from their soccer camp. Laughing at me, he knew what I was thinking. Calling his mother back was not my point. He smiled and assured me that my sons were having a good time and that they were fine and happy. I knew he was talking about himself too, and the gesture was well appreciated.

Besides, he told me, "The call is more of a follow-up from our visit earlier in the day — nothing that I need to worry about." Apparently that was how communication worked between families living in Ireland and the States.

As we talked about the boys and Michael's relationship with his mom, he told me he sent her the picture we had taken on the day we met. Being the sharp woman I knew she was, she asked him if we were in a hotel room.

"Oh my God, Michael! How could you have sent that picture? Now she must think we slept together and I'm a tramp," I said with the "I could kill you" tone in my voice. I thanked God that I had decided not to visit him on the same weekend as his mother.

"My mother is not stupid, and we are forty-four-year-old adults, Kimberly," he said, implying that being in a hotel room would have been normal after first meeting.

Rolling my eyes at him, I explained that being his mother's only beloved son meant that no girl would ever be good enough for him, never mind someone whose first impression was that she was a tramp. All the fantasies I had of one day visiting County Offaly were being stomped out as I explained that to him. His amusement showed on his face, prompting me to take another picture of him, preserving the first time I wanted to kill him.

Later in the evening, Michael took me, via Google Earth, to his home in Ireland. As we traveled through his small town on the laptop, he told me every detail about Geashill. He showed me his parents' tavern, where everyone gathered to discuss the latest football and hurling results, and the Catholic church he, his mother, and his sisters attended (but never his father). He showed me the athletic field and the petrol station where he'd worked during the summers as a teen.

He told me the names and histories of the families who settled the town long before his parents moved there. Moving through the streets and out into the country, he showed me a piece of land he wanted to buy and build a house on. There was an old country house already on the property. It was built long ago in the traditional Irish-style white rectangle with a high-pitched roof. He planned to tear it down and build something new. It was then that Michael discovered my love for history. I savored anything old and authentic. "Michael, that is what makes this piece of land wonderful — its history. You have to keep that house and build something wonderful to match it."

"Kimberly, do you know how thick those walls are?" he said. As a carpenter, I'm sure he could easily see the challenge in saving the old house and building another to match, but he let me enjoy my fantasy, appreciating my enthusiasm. "Okay, then we will work around it. You shall keep your chilly, old barricade, and I will live in the new quarters with air conditioning and heat." His answer turned my pout into a smile. I enjoyed the thought of living with him in such a beautiful place.

That night while he showered, I packed my suitcase. I pulled out a blank card that I had brought with me to leave for him. I had selected a card without any words on purpose, knowing I would feel the right thing to say after we spent time together. I was right. I did know what to say. I opened the card and neatly wrote:

> *Michael, I came without expectations and an open heart, and I am leaving without expectations and an open heart. But I now know what I came to find out. You are a good man. Thank you for everything.*
> *All My Love,*
> *Kimberly*

We went to bed early. At peace once again in his embrace, I drifted to sleep. The alarm came early and I awoke alone. I found Michael asleep on the sofa. His shoulders had been bothering him after wrecking his bike and falling from scaffolding only a few days after he began working. He still had pain and couldn't sleep very well sometimes. Showered, dressed, and ready to leave, I debated whether I should wake him up or not. I wanted him to sleep, knowing he was restless that night, but walking away from him without saying goodbye would make it as though our time together had vanished like a morning fog. Bending down, I kissed his lips. His response was instant and hungry. He grabbed me and pulled me to him. We moved as reflections of each other in our need to be together and our desire to possess and control each other, if only for those last few moments. His lust gave way to love as my love gave way to lust, and we crossed over to another place where we were whole again.

Rising to make me some morning tea, he kissed me and thanked me for waking him before leaving. "Most girls would have just left without saying goodbye." His smile gave way to an Irish smirk. He cocked his eyebrow, which put a ridiculous grin on my face. I regained my composure, got dressed, and became aware of the time again.

I walked to the front window and saw the car had arrived to take me to the airport. "The car is here," I said, with a knot in my throat. Leaving the tea he was making, Michael met me halfway across the room. Fighting my rising emotions, I gave him a quick, unceremonious kiss and whispered, "I love you." Turning before he could wrap his arms around me, I bolted out the door, bags and shoes in hand. I dove into the back seat of the car, not wanting to look back as the driver took me off into the dark morning. But I did. Michael and I watched each other until the car disappeared around the corner. Grateful for the open window splashing my face with cool northern air, soothing my stinging eyes, I sat back and let the tears roll down my face.

• • •

My father picked me up from the airport. The flight was only two-and-a-half hours and seemed way too fast. The reality of going back to my "normal" life was shocking. The now familiar feeling of leaving home, rather than going home, overwhelmed me. I sat in the passenger seat of the truck in silence, leaving my dad uncomfortable. Normally I would have indulged him with all the excitement from my trip, but the trip was not exciting. It was real — so real that I wasn't quite sure how I was going to fit back into my world without Michael again.

Dad finally broke the silence. "So, did you have a good time?"

"Yes," I answered without any details.

"Do you think you will see him again?" Pushing me further.

I answered, "Yes, I hope so." Changing the subject, I asked how everyone was at home. As Dad gave me the rundown of the past few days, I realized how different time actually felt when I was with Michael. Every moment seemed expanded, richer, and more valuable than the typical routine at home. Yes, being in the present moment while I was with Michael gave me more time than the days on the calendar actually showed.

My only contact with Michael was once again by way of the phone. It made me ache for him — his body, his face, his eyes, and his animation when he talked. He told me he ran into Leland's sister-in-law again, whom I'd met at the pub. He was surprised to see her again so soon. It had been years since they had seen one another. The first thing she said was, "How is Kimberly?"

Having not spoken to me yet, he told her he did not know but hoped I was home safe. "I think you left as good of an impression on Brooklyn as you did on me."

I laughed and asked, "Exactly what impression was that?"

"You're easy to be with, Kimberly. You put everyone at ease, especially me," he said with a gentle seriousness. "You don't seem to notice how everyone watches you. You actually light up a room when you are there."

"But Michael, it was you they were all happy to see. Everyone loves you, and if I was beaming, it was because I was with you," I said in a sexy, playful tone, remembering all the random people smiling at us as we passed by and how happy everyone seemed when we spent time talking with them. Perhaps it was our joy that was reflected back at us, or maybe just our love for each other was enough for everyone to feel too.

Switching the tone, he said, "I hope you really had a good time."

"I did," I promised.

What he didn't understand was that I saw him in the exact environment that I wanted to see him in. I found a man who picked up my chunk of fresh baguette, buttered it, and handed it back to me as if he had done it for years. I found a guy who was loved by his family and friends, someone who could make a new friend wherever he went. I found a man who could tell me with his eyes that the next stop on the subway was ours. I found a man I could live with every day and never, ever stop smiling about how magnificent it was that I created our meeting. I discovered he was a good man. I got to share three more perfect days, and none of it was about doing. It was about *being* — being together as one.

CHAPTER NINE

COMING HOME TO MY HEART

In the hero's journey, there is a return home to the ordinary world. Michael was my reward after facing a challenge I had set my quest to achieve. With the validation and celebration now over, perhaps the most difficult part of the journey lay before me.

Michael and I settled into a routine of talking on the phone every night, sometimes into the early morning hours or until our phone batteries died — whichever happened first. Michael would be sitting under the Verrazano Bridge while I was lying in bed wishing he were next to me. I was missing him and missing being where he was. I was comforted when he shared the details of his days with me, which now became so much richer having experienced them myself.

We were also changing our habits for the better. Michael, a reformed smoker — though you would never know because of his patience and support for those around him who still smoked — was surprised at how little I did smoke around him. In fact, when I was in New York, I actually forgot to smoke almost entirely. So when I took a Theta healing certificate program two weeks after my return, that was the first thing I went to work on for myself. I officially became a nonsmoker.

Michael was going through his own evolution, opting to replace his nightly routine at the pub filled with beer and merriment with riding his bike every day. He would explore the city riding over the Brooklyn Bride and through Manhattan. It was making him physically strong and healthy again. Inspired by his actions, I joined my father during his daily ten-mile bike rides.

We were good for each other. Without the need or desire to push one another, we were simply inspired and supportive of each other. We began to make business plans together. We settled on quitting smoking as our first teachable program. I was also teaching Infinite Possibilities — the program we learned together. Michael knew how much I loved it. He gave me the strength to face a class I was about to teach at a food bank. I'd taught the program many times to teens on the soccer field, but this was different. I was frustrated trying to get the program perfect, and I kept getting stuck. Just as I was starting to panic, Michael asked me what was bothering me. "Well, all this 'change your thoughts, change your life' stuff is great, but will it really help a guy who doesn't have a place to live and can't feed himself?" I answered him with the questions I was asking myself, making me rethink everything. "This work is more valuable than anything I have ever done. Can I really help these people? What am I going to say to change their lives?" There, I said it — the truth of my lack of faith in the law of attraction.

"You will inspire them with stories about people who have made it, who have changed their lives, and how they can do it too." He sounded so sure. "Kimberly, I know the only reason this is frightening you is because this is truly what your gift is."

He was right. He had been his own version of Robin Hood in England where he had to work in order to make a good living. He understood my worries, and he loved that it meant so much to me to make a real difference in the world.

One of the things I loved about the way we did things together was the polarity in which we approached a subject. I was always gentler, more esoteric, and spiritual. He was more scientific, driven by research and truth. We knew and trusted each other. We knew that no matter what we did together, it would be successful.

Michael had a business background in sales and marketing products, and my life was spent in branding and marketing. Together, our minds and experience created a successful program for people who needed to quit smoking. Our focus was to start in the European market — one he knew well. I was excited to work with him. This was part of the manifestation I called forth — to work together with my partner helping people understand their own power and value.

Even though we were having fun working on our program together and sharing our lives day by day, not having him present was difficult. I was ready for him to come to see me in my world. I wanted him to come to Florida and see me before he returned to England. However, he was very clear with me that he needed to return prior to visiting Florida in order to move his belongings out of his apartment and take them home to Ireland. But I had a feeling that once he left, he would never return. He needed to see my life before we could move forward with the possibility of a life together, one that would inevitably lead to Ireland.

Every week I would inquire whether he made plans to return to England. His answer was always no. I knew this was because he was unsure of what he wanted in his big-picture plans, but it was also because it was his natural tendency to not plan ahead of time in any great detail. I was a Virgo, which makes me a plan maker, but loving Michael meant trusting him in all things, even if it meant not having the answers I wanted. I was also a mom, and moms like plans, schedules, and organization, but the freedom Michael was accustomed to without the responsibility of children and a wife left him unaffected by my weekly worrying.

Knowing that the Olympics were coming soon and that they were being held in London meant flying during that time could be a concern. Michael agreed that it could not only be costly but it would be safer when the world wasn't focused on one place. So for the next foreseeable month, it was unlikely he could get to England and then Ireland. And that meant it would be months before I saw him again.

Finally my patience wore thin, and I gave in to my own need to see him at the risk of pissing him off. He already told me clearly that he could not come to see me until he made a trip home. On top of that, I knew he was once annoyed with a pushy ex-girlfriend who booked a trip for him against his wishes. I booked a flight for him anyway, remembering his text to me that had read "just come."

In a carefully crafted email, I explained:

> Hello Beloved Michael,
>
> You told me that if I have any intuitive insights to things that you would like to hear them. Well, my love, I know it is important for you to "just come."
>
> I realize you do usually seem to respond well when I take over ;) so I hope you will take this with that spirit of adventure and fun instead of being upset with me for doing it.
>
> I love you. I do hope to see you next Friday night. If you are still pissed at me by then, you can spank me ;) I think you might like that too.
>
> Xoxo
> Kimberly
> Attached is your flight schedule.

Then I waited, checking my phone regularly for a reply. At ten o'clock, I got the usual text message: "Babes are you still up?" So I called him.

"Hi, babe. Are you still at the house, or are you out?" I asked, knowing he usually left the house to call me.

He hadn't left yet, and I decided I needed to fess up and at the very least get my worry over with. I asked him to check his email from me, quickly adding that I thought I might have stepped over the line. When he asked me why I thought that, I could tell by his tone that he was a bit concerned.

I dove in with reference to the books I had been reading and sharing with him, *Fifty Shades of Grey*. "Well ..." I stalled for a second, gathering my strategy. "I want you to know I did something that I know was against your plan, and I know you don't like to be controlled or manipulated, but I want you to know you are completely in control. It is your decision if you want to do this or not. So I *will* understand if you choose not to."

While I was giving my sales pitch, or rather defense pitch, he was opening his laptop and had my email on his screen.

"My itinerary? What's this?" His voice seemed softer now but still guarded.

He read my words aloud, and I could hear the low sound of a smirk coming from somewhere deep inside him. Good — I had written it well.

"Friday night?" he questioned.

"Michael, I booked you a flight to come see me. I thought you could use a getaway, and I want you to come before you go back to Europe. I hope you're not pissed." I could almost hear the begging in my own voice.

His response, as always, reassured me that everything was all right and in divine order. "Why would I be pissed? You bought me a ticket to Florida to see you. Miss me, do you?" The lightness returned to his voice. "Yippee, hooray! I'll see you soon, then." His yippees and hoorays always amused me coming from such a strong, big man. I did not know whether it was his Irish heritage or younger self coming out, but it always made me happy.

It was set. The following weekend, I would have this man who amazed me in *my* life, and I was ready to share it with him.

• • •

In the days prior to Michael's arrival, the thrill of him coming to see me became more agonizing than the trip planning to see him in New York. All my friends wanted to meet the man who at last turned my head. To be totally honest, they were all aware — maybe more so than me — that his existence had given me the joy that each one longed for me to have.

My parents, of course, were anxious to meet him. I asked my mother to make dinner for us, but the plan somehow quickly jumped from an intimate family dinner to a party with all of her friends, who also wanted to meet him. I was a wreck — and aware of my secret selfish desire to keep him all to myself. I was starting to regret telling anyone he was coming at all.

The boys had their own agenda, and so did their friends. As kids of a single mom who never normally goes on dates and usually has a house full of kids and always gives them love advice, lectures, and support, they were more than happy to reciprocate.

Pathetically, I probably needed the advice, but I opted to put my foot down to only allow my sons' nearest and dearest friends over while Michael was at our house. I agreed that we would attend their soccer games, which thankfully were in town that weekend. I also told them they were allowed to invite him to play soccer, but that they were to make sure to not cause him any harm. He was still not fully recovered from his acrobatics on his bike and scaffolding. I made it perfectly clear that this was my weekend to have fun, and for once they needed to accommodate me. They were more amused than anything and took every opportunity to tease me about the things they were conjuring up to embarrass me.

To make things worse, Hurricane Isaac was headed our way.

The Thursday before he was to fly in, I had to tell him the situation. "Michael, you might not want to come tomorrow. If you do, I can almost guarantee you will not be returning home on Monday. We have a hurricane coming Sunday night, and they will shut down the airport for sure."

Almost — but not completely — surprising me, he replied, "I haven't been through a hurricane before. It will be a new experience. Besides, I can help you clean up if you need it. So if I can't get back because of the storm for a few days, what can they say?" This man was really too good to be true.

All things were right again. I wondered why I ever let myself get off center. Not one time had Michael ever disappointed me. Not one time had he not soothed my ruffled feathers, no matter the subject. He always believed in me, propped me up, and urged me forward. He communicated openly and freely about matters of his heart, mind, and soul. I could feel him and play with his energy even though we were 1,000 miles apart. Our time together was going to be fabulous. I relaxed and started counting down the hours, texting him every now and then to let him know how soon we would be together.

• • •

While driving to the airport and rounding a bend in the road that ran parallel to the runway, I saw the Jet Blue logo on the tail of the plane as it was landing. He was here! Before the plane even turned off the runway to the gate, a text popped up on my phone: "Yippee, yahoo, and hurray! I am here. XX." Michael was just as excited as I was.

As I was waiting for my ticket into the parking garage, I quickly texted back: "I saw you land. Are you still on the plane?"

He responded with a "yes xxx."

Good. I had plenty of time to park and be in the terminal by the time he came out of the concourse.

Have you ever been so excited — I mean really excited, the jump-up-and-down, squealing, body-jerking excited — like kids get in anticipation of something wonderful? I had only experienced this type of excitement a few times as an adult, but it usually stemmed from something incredible, like when one of my boys was about to win a state championship in soccer.

As I quickly made my way through the airport, I felt the anticipation of seeing Michael take over every cell in my body. I tried to contain myself from actually jumping up and down right in the middle of everyone, and it occurred to me that this was the first time I felt this way about seeing him. When I traveled to New York to visit him, I was approaching the trip with a "who is this man?" mindset. This time, he was my man, and bringing him home to my family and into my world was the beginning of our life together.

As I searched every face coming through the gate, I finally saw him emerge from the crowd, exiting past security. I didn't move. I was frozen, struck by how incredibly handsome he was. He stood just over six feet tall with his broad shoulders. Even at a distance, his eyes were dramatic and powerful. Dressed in all black, his T-shirt fit tight against his chest and arms. He had grown a full beard since I had seen him last, and it suited him. I smiled, noticing how sexy his European look was. He was mine, the One I had been looking for my whole life. As I watched him take in the tropical scenery of the airport, I called out to him, but my voice did not sound like my voice. His eyes found me and reflected back my smile. Everything disappeared around us, and at that moment, we were both in the here and now *and* in another time and place.

All at once, I witnessed another time when we had come together. The light giving way to long shadows dancing and reflecting off of the river beside me told me it was fall. He had come home after being away for a long time. His walk toward me was steady and strong, taking me in as he approached me as if asking permission to have me again. His clothes were hand hewn and his hair long and curly. His beard was trimmed short, hiding his face, but his eyes, those eyes, were Michael's. Slowly, he dropped his bag and reached for me, smelling my golden hair and kissing me hard on my forehead. Suddenly I was wrapped in his arms, my face flushed with the anticipation of another kiss, and we were again in Fort Myers. The sounds of people and airplanes replaced the sound of nature's silence. I was in his arms once again, and all was calm, peaceful, and right with the world. Arm in arm, we left the airport.

As anxious as I was to see Michael, my sons seemed to reflect the same anxiousness. This man had my heart, something they never remembered sharing. I knew they wanted to like him as much as I did, but their criteria for having a man in our lives was much different from my own. I didn't worry about it. I knew their happiness in a relationship with a man was a big part of what I asked from the Universe. I wanted a family, not just a man. Michael was a male version of myself, and I knew they would do just fine together. When we arrived home to meet the boys, Michael had the same ease that had captured my attention.

• • •

Michael came into the kitchen after putting his bags upstairs. Wrapping his arms around me from behind, he kissed my temple and said, "When you talk about the boys, maybe you should speak about them as young men."

"What do you mean?" I said, happy that my world was now one.

"I know they are your world, but you have raised two very fine, funny, and well-adjusted young men. They seem to see you as a woman and not just their mother. Perhaps you can relax knowing how wise they are and that they are young men and not just your babies." He turned me around, smiling at me with a sense of pride.

"Dear lord, what did they say to you?" I raised an eyebrow in anticipation of God-knows-what.

"No worries," he said, laughing. "But from what I know about you, their advice seems pretty accurate," he said, showing off his insatiable Irish smirk.

I packed a bottle of wine and two glasses into a picnic basket and handed it to him. "Here. Let's go." I said, rolling my eyes and picking up the blankets I had ready.

"Where are we going already?" he asked, looking quizzical.

"It's a surprise," I said, winking at him.

The approaching hurricane had cooled the night air and stirred the usually calm Gulf of Mexico, which was now beating roughly against the shore of Sanibel Island's Lighthouse Point. We were alone; even the stars were tucked in under the cloud cover, reminding me of Rockaway. Only the distant lights of Estero Island could be seen. We talked for hours, as we were accustomed to do, but tonight, there was more than just the night sky connecting us. We were wrapped up together in blankets, me resting in his arms, as a comfortable silence warmed with wine stirred my imagination. Was the vision at the airport of his return home from a distant place real? Had we truly been together and separated before? If it was real, perhaps that was why I so strongly felt the need to have him come "home" to me. I wondered whether there were more visions yet to reveal other lifetimes together. I let myself drift to Ireland, wondering how soon it would be when we could be there on the shore, listening to the sound of crashing waves. I wondered whether he too knew we were one, meeting once again.

At home in the warmth of the shower, he kissed my wet hair, his body resting against mine. We were silent, communicating only with our thoughts and bodies. Our words became too cumbersome, too tiring, and not necessary. The steam of the shower protected and insulated us from all else, letting us exist beyond the boundaries of our physical realities. He was home again.

• • •

The plan was for Michael to meet my parents after a few days of acclimation, but my mother's preparation for Hurricane Ivan woke us early the next morning. I decided to check the news to see what we were dealing with, and what I saw dampened my spirit. We were still smack in the center of the dreaded cone of uncertainty. Even though Michael had asked me not to make any real plans, I still wanted to show him the highlights of southwest Florida. That possibility was quickly fading with the bands of Ivan moving in.

Normal life, or at least normal life under a hurricane, would prevail, and there was work to be done around the house. Accepting in my mind that all things happen for a reason, I tossed his clothes at him and invited him to join me on my morning bike ride. I was now riding every day, but my route was nowhere near the trek that he was used to in the city. At least I was active again, and this morning's option of hiding under the covers with him and watching the world go by had already gone by the wayside.

Arriving at my parents' house at the end of our wind-blown bike ride, I gave him a "here we go" smile as my mom came out to meet us. I wasn't nervous for him or me. I knew he would easily win my mother's heart with his ease, quick wit, and beautiful face. However, it was his Irish brogue that put a smile on her face when he greeted her. Michael possessed the same emotional intelligence as my oldest son. They both had the ability to put anyone they came across at ease. It was a trait I both admired and found humorous. It was also something I loved to watch.

On the other hand, I was very nervous about my father meeting Michael. For some reason, it seemed like a big deal for him to meet my father. I knew my dad was looking forward to meeting him. He already respected any man who was strong enough to not only "handle me" — his words, not mine — but sweep me off to another country, as well. Days before Michael arrived, my father had told me, "I have been thinking about this whole thing. This could really work. You only have a few years before both boys will be graduating high school, and even though they will be in college, we will be there to help and support them." I was impressed that my father knew me so well that I did not even have to tell him what my thoughts were. I was happy he gave me permission, though I did not feel like I needed it. This was a big deal, and the meeting of the two men in my life was important to me.

Once I was inside the house, I introduced the two of them and left them on their own while I went to help my mother go through the necessary checklist of things she needed done to be ready for the hurricane. The men only talked for a few minutes, discussing Dad's recent fall, reconstructive surgery, recovery strategy, and what "man things" needed to be done for the approaching storm that my father could not do in his situation. However, I sensed they both seemed to understand their mutual desire for my happiness. It surprised me how easy it was for them to just get to the point, establish what needed to be done, and move on. Women usually need more time to get to know each other. I hoped that if I ever met his mother, it would go just as well.

Besides Michael's ease with people, I was also learning that he had an incredible level of patience. My mother kept us busy moving things outside to keep them from crashing through her windows. Her nervousness about not putting up the metal panels on the windows and doors and turning her house into a soup can was making her take extra precautions. I was vacillating between worry about how ready I was for the storm and how ridiculous it was for us to be moving planters that took two people to move. It was wearing on my patience. Michael, on the other hand, seemed completely fine. With my mother's last instructions to go to the gas station and fill the gas containers "exactly" three-quarters full so that they would not spill, and to make sure that we did not fill them in the back of the truck because it could ignite a fire, I was sent over the edge. Trying to end the conversation, I said, "Mom, Michael's uncle owned a petrol station all his life. He knows." Both my mom and Michael seemed to be unaffected by my impatience. He was a good man — a much better man than I was a daughter.

• • •

I hoped he would be as at ease at my home as I was having him there, and over the next day, we took care of our own Ivan preparation with Michael in charge. Being together just seemed so natural, almost as if we were a couple who'd been living together in harmony for years. Knowing each other's ways already, we were able to be together yet still not be attached every moment.

Michael found his way to my computer. He spent hours downloading all available information that he thought I would be interested in from European websites that the U.S. didn't have to offer, at least not for free. He figured out on his own how to operate my Mac computer without any help from me or the boys. Any question he asked about the computer was answered by the "I have no idea" kind of statements, leaving him alone to figure it out. Technology was not my thing, but fortunately it was his. Patiently, he showed me step by step what he did for me and taught me how to access everything I could ever need or want to download for free. No wonder he was such a good researcher; information and reports were available that you could never find using Google. It occurred to me that his patience with teaching me must have come from living with three sisters. One way or another, he explained it to me and made sure I understood, despite my lack of interest in learning it.

Our true partnership resonated in the way we carried on conversations with others. We easily agreed on the plans we made for the boys and ourselves. He even overrode my opinion one night when the boys were pleading their case about going to a rival high school to watch their school's team play against them. He was such a natural at making me feel like I didn't need to be on guard or justify how I felt as he pled the boys' case right alongside them, all the while wrapping himself around me, assuring me all was well. When I finally gave in to some rather logical points that Michael made in his case, the boys ran off doing a victory celebration dance about their newly formed bromance with the Irish jock.

"So were you trying to win points or trying to get me alone?" I asked playfully after the boys left for the night.

He laughed. "Neither. I was supporting a good cause, but the results seem to have benefited me in both ways," he said, smirking and pulling me down next to him to watch an Irish chick flick movie he'd found earlier that day.

When the movie was over, Michael went upstairs as I put away the dishes and let the dogs out one last time before bed. Looking into the fast-moving clouds with the stars peeking through every so often, I thought about the times before when I looked out and felt lonely. I thought how strange it was that now when I looked out, I felt connected again. I was at home both with Michael and in my heart. I smiled and blew the universe a kiss before I shut the door.

My heart melted as I walked into the bedroom to find Michael lighting the last of the candles we'd gathered in case the power went out. "I guess you are not too worried about being in the dark tomorrow night?" I said, smiling in appreciation of his romantic nature.

"I would be perfectly happy in a dark cave with you, but tonight we are going to enjoy the harvest of every drawer and pantry you have, Kimberly," he proclaimed, bowing to me.

"My Lord, you have done a splendid job sweeping this American girl off her feet! How is it that you possess such talents and skills?" I said in my best English accent.

With all seriousness, looking deeply into my eyes, he asked, "Have I swept you off your feet?"

"Yes," I said, not letting go of his gaze.

Piece by piece, he undressed me, letting my clothes drop to the floor. I did not move; I did not look away from his captivating eyes. Naked before him, I let go, willing everything I had to him, letting him make love to me in a sensuous, delicious, and slow way.

• • •

The next morning with the storm about to arrive, I checked in with the airline to see whether they had canceled Michael's flight yet. Living in a place that often falls inside of the hurricanes' cones of doom, this is fairly commonplace, right along with food and household preparations. The agent told me that the flight had not been canceled yet but then asked me to hold for a moment. Within a minute, a supervisor was on the line asking if I wanted to reschedule now, because they were expecting all flights on the west coast of Florida to be canceled within the hour. I knew it, and I felt guilty about how pleased I was to hear the news. I called out to Michael, asking him when he would like to leave — or if he would like to stay a month or possibly forever. He laughed but then chose the evening flight two days later. I knew he had to get back to work, but he didn't choose the earliest flight available, either, which made me smile.

"I am happy we have more time," I said, hanging up the phone, "but I meant it when I teased you about staying a month or much, much longer." I could tell by the look on his face that he knew I meant it. I also knew that if he thought he could have stayed without letting down his coworkers in New York, he would have. The weatherman's hurricane cone of doom had bought us another two days together.

That night, we had dinner at my parents' house. What was expected to be a night full of wind and storm was calm and breezy. With only my family's dearest and oldest friends Betty Ann and Jeff in attendance, I was at ease and spent the night as an observer watching the joy everyone felt for me. I watched Michael entertain everyone with his charm and storytelling. He even managed to sneak a drink to my father, thinking it went under my mother's radar. Since my father's fall from a ladder while trimming the trees, my mother had been my father's dutiful wound-care specialist and strict nurse, administering his IV antibiotics perfectly as prescribed by his doctors. Alcohol was not part of the protocol, and I knew she did not miss it. However, my father enjoyed the drink, and it seemed to be a guy bonding thing, much like the traditional Irish pub "I'll buy a round; you buy a round" custom. Dinner was wonderful, and Michael was duly impressed with my mother's talents in the kitchen and her ability to embarrass me with her stories of my teenage antics.

After we left to go home, I never thought to call and check in with my parents to see what they thought of him. It didn't seem to matter to me; I didn't feel the need to get their feedback.

• • •

Looking back in my life, I cannot remember a time when I was not on the path of awakening. Some of my earliest memories were not about my friends or a typical life but about my relationship to things unseen. There were periods in my life when I tried to blend in and be "normal," but like most of us on this path, in my own heart I felt different. When I was very young, I thought it was normal to interact with the realm beyond, but over the years, I discovered that in order to be socially accepted, people were expected to turn off or simply ignore such gifts.

Throughout the years, teachers showed up as I was ready to awaken to more, yet I still carefully guarded these different parts of myself. When I met Michael, I knew that he could see me and everything I was. The intimacy this brought between us was immediate. The walls we normally build to protect ourselves from pain did not exist between Michael and me.

There wasn't anything we needed from each other to fulfill a need that we could not meet within ourselves. No thoughts of shame or worry existed. The only desire we had was to experience more of each other. We became each other's teachers and students, expanding our minds and understanding of spirituality and relearning what physical love was without veils of the ego. The freedom we found losing ourselves in each other's desires awakened us to the holiness of union between our two bodies. For the first time in my life, I loved my body as he loved it. And he knew of my love for his body, which only made him feel stronger and more alive.

• • •

The day Michael was leaving, we got up early to go kayaking. The storm had passed without any significance. It moved further up the Gulf Coast and looked as if it would terrorize New Orleans again. The river was high. We were the first ones to enter the park that had been closed due to the impending weather, giving us the peace we needed to enjoy our last hours together.

As I had in New York, I let Michael take control. It was something I was not used to doing in my environment, but for those few hours, I let go and let him guide us down the river. We talked about the perfection we found in our intimacy and the gentle way we healed one another. I found him at the perfect moment in my life, and he felt the same about me. "Nothing exists between us; we are two sides to the same coin," he said, holding his hand out and turning it over to illustrate.

Our awareness of what we gave each other without any fear seemed natural yet in striking contrast to what we learned before. Michael was vaguely aware I was abused in my marriage, but it wasn't until now that I shared the details with him. He needed to know, and I needed to let go of my fears of intimacy that had guided my behavior over the years. It was there in the park that we shed our final fears about our imperfections, standing face-to-face, acknowledging and letting go of words that could never be uttered to another before. It was there in the park that my heart broke just a little for us not having found each other sooner and for having to carry that weight in our hearts for as long as we did. It was there in the park that we found the perfection of our reflections whole and healthy.

CHAPTER TEN

YOU DON'T COMPLETE ME

You can never get it wrong. It is never complete, and all is exactly as it should be. And that is the part of this reality that sucks.

Slamming on my brakes in the afternoon's mad dash to pick up my son from school, I pulled myself back into my physical reality, narrowly missing another car and the chance to exchange personal information with a complete stranger. I was lost for a moment, listening intently on the car's speakerphone to Michael's Irish accent with the *tr*'s instead of *th*'s. I was not really listening to what he was saying, but simply enjoying the sound of his voice as I carefully navigated my way through traffic into a less hectic direction. I realized that he was trying to recite a famous line from a movie when I decided to rejoin the conversation.

"That's from the movie with Tom Cruise — the one where he is the 'show me the money' character that represents professional sports players." I jumped in, trying to help him get to the point. "Remember? He said to her, 'You complete me,' so then she said, 'Shut up. You had me at hello.'"

"Yes, yes, yes, that's the one!" Michael said, relieved that I was now on the same page with him.

"Michael, you had me from hello too, you know," I said with complete sincerity.

He hesitated for just a moment. "I did?"

I was always surprised by his doubt in our connection. Even after witnessing it myself so many times before, I knew he was just reflecting my own vulnerability, needing to be loved and being afraid of not having this wonderful thing that we cocreated together.

Regaining his train of thought, he tried to correct me. "Kimberly, you are complete. You don't need someone else to complete you."

"You're right. I don't, and that's the point. I *am* complete." My mind flashed back to his hotel room in Orlando when I so miserably failed in my attempt to explain to him why I did not date. I told him I did not want to be the teacher in the relationship, and I knew he didn't understand me. I used this new opportunity as an opening to explain an intimate part of myself. "Michael, remember when you asked me how could I know that I loved you?"

"Yes," he said slowly.

I took a breath and tried to explain more clearly than I had before. "It is because I have learned how to love myself first. I know I am complete with just myself and God, but loving you expands me. It's not a question of *if* you are someone I can love. Loving you brings expansion to me. I love you so easily because I love myself. Because we resonate so closely together, and because we are so similar in so many ways, loving you is totally natural. The love I have for you just expands my love of me. That's why I can't date just anyone. That is why when I met you I knew instantly — because I felt the expansion inside of me. I loved myself more after I met you, and I could see myself in you. So there has never been a doubt in my mind that I love you. Does that make sense to you? I don't need you to complete me. I love you, and I always will — endlessly."

The shock in his voice told me he understood. He replied, "That doesn't leave you many people to date. There are not very many people in the world who can understand that and not just take from you."

"You're right, and that is why I end up in a teacher role so often," I said, relieved that I was finally able to understand it myself and in turn verbalize it to another person.

• • •

Michael and I had been through a rough few weeks. Or at least I had. He was having phone issues again, which made me really frustrated with him. He was frustrated with his work situation and the lack of work since returning from Florida. I was happy to know that at least he was working with people he really enjoyed. Our circumstances seemed to be showing me that we were together, reflecting each other. We were both aware that we were in this together, that we were there for each other.

Or so I thought.

Just a week before, my father was admitted back into the hospital to be immediately treated for a life-threatening infection that resulted from the surgery after his fall from the ladder. The call I received from my mother about the severity of the situation was very upsetting and frightening. I called Michael as soon as I got off the phone with her. He did not answer again. I hadn't heard from him in over twenty-four hours. Dialing him again and again, I was getting nowhere. I was angry at myself for both wanting him and knowing that no matter how many times I called, he wasn't going to answer.

I wanted him to tell me that this was going to be all right. I knew he would understand my panic, having unexpectedly lost his father just a few months earlier. I needed him to be there. I was angry that my dad was the one person I had always turned to before and now he was the one I could be losing. I needed Michael to tell me I was "ten feet tall and bulletproof," as he always did when I was feeling like a panicked little girl. Before I went into the hospital to see my father, I paced in front of the entrance and decided to call a much-needed friend. Steve answered immediately, and I blurted out, "I need you!"

"What's wrong?" he said. I felt him stop everything and shift his attention completely onto me.

I wanted to answer, "What is wrong is that you are on the phone and not Michael!" But instead of letting that come out of my mouth, I chose to say as calmly as possible, "They have admitted my father into the hospital. He has an infection, and my mother said he could lose his leg or die. Can you do something?"

Steve was my teacher when I took the Theta healing course over the summer. We had become very good friends. Being the amazingly gifted healer he was, he went right to work — not on my dad, but on me. Instantly, I could feel the calmness and love spreading throughout my entire body.

"Okay, I can feel that. Thank you, Steve," I said. "Can you focus your work on my father now?"

"I already am," he replied happily, and with that I received the reassurance I was looking for.

In the following days that my father was in the hospital, I came to the realization that I did not need Michael but that I wanted him. I wanted him to be my hero, to lie to me if needed, to make me believe that everything was in divine order and that all was well. Now that I had made it through the anxiety and panic without him, I came to the realization that wanting him somehow seemed harder for me to admit than needing him.

After three days of not hearing from Michael, his phone finally began working again. All of a sudden, receiving a happy-face text message from his number did not please me. In fact, it upset me. I responded to his text with, "Michael, you need to know I'm struggling. I have stepped over my own boundary and allowed myself to need someone. I have not even allowed myself to emotionally need my own family, but I needed you — so much."

The next text I sent read, "Michael, they are taking my dad in for emergency surgery."

His reply came two hours later. It said, "My thoughts and well wishes are with you & your family for your dad. Universal healing energy from me to your dad. XX."

The problem with texting, or any nonverbal communication, is the lack of emotion that words don't convey on their own. It leaves the person who receives the text message to view the tone of the message based on his or her own frame of mind, which is never a good thing in emotional situations. Obviously, being in a weak state of mind, I took his text as a rather cold cop-out. I visualized him feeling like a dog with his tail between his legs for not being there for me. Then I visualized him looking at his phone thinking that I was some dramatic whack job. Neither vision gave me the warmth and support I so desperately wanted from him. I replied to him explaining that I was not really expecting him to come to my rescue but that I also wanted him to understand where I was mentally and what I was feeling. I then added, "Thanks. Please just tell me it's going to be all right."

His call came a few minutes later. His Irish brogue filled me, thawing me a bit and telling me exactly what I already knew but did not have the strength to believe on my own. We each create our own realities — my father, his father, and even me. My heart ached that I could have possibly created a reality that might not include my father. I insisted that Michael lie to me if necessary, allowing me to believe and feel that everything was going to be fine. I wanted to hold on to the vibration of well-being that somehow was impossible for me to muster on my own. I heard him walk the fine line of truth and faith. He was good at that. He understood, and he was my hero in that moment.

• • •

My father safely made it through his second surgery, and life began to have a routine again. One evening waiting for my boys in the parking lot of their school's stadium, I felt like I could breathe again. I heard cheers coming from the fans in the football game, and I smiled, knowing that the Vikings scored a touchdown.

That feeling reminded me of how Michael could always calm and center me, even before I knew him as the amazing physical being he was. This night was no different. As I pondered and appreciated the night, my life, and Michael, I felt a shift. I was at ease again, and I was no longer annoyed with myself for wanting him. It was normal and healthy for me to want someone I loved so much, someone who would answer with truth and love, despite my desperate pleas to just fix everything. This was the relationship I had dreamed of my whole life.

I mentally wrapped my heart around him as he sat 1,200 miles away from me under a bridge where he always talked to me.

• • •

I asked Michael to catch me up on the past few days. He shared how his heart was breaking over the dysfunction in the family he was living with and how difficult his living situation had become. Although it was none of my business how his friend Leland's relationship was falling apart, being in a new relationship, I could not keep myself from witnessing and judging the insanity — at least in terms of how I would choose to behave in their situation. Michael, on the other hand, was fairer in his opinion of the situation, and with him having been so close to the family in which it was happening, I knew he wished he could do something to change it. Our exchange discussing someone else's life over the next few minutes changed ours.

Actually a bit puzzled over his compassion for Leland's wife, I stopped him and said, "Michael, if you went into the hospital like Leland did last weekend, I would be on the next plane to New York. I wouldn't just ignore the situation. And we have only just started this relationship."

He hesitated as he always did when I surprised him. "You would?"

"Yes, I would!" I replied with complete seriousness.

Michael answered me softly and slowly. "I just told my mother when I was speaking with her that I might have to return to Florida if something happened to your father. I would get myself there as soon as I could, to be there for you … and your family."

Realizing what he was saying on so many levels, I told him the truth — "you might have to" — leaving us in silence again.

Driving home with the boys, listening to them reliving the ups and downs of being fans of a losing football team, I replayed my conversation with Michael in my mind. He and I came together completely, without hesitation. He knew me more than I imagined someone could. He knew my heart and soul, and I knew his, even though we were not experiencing the daily details of life in person. I felt so loved. I was filled with peace and appreciation for the life that I cocreated with him.

There is an ease that comes when two people have let go of their fear of each other. It's a natural awareness of each other whether you are in one another's presence or not. I have witnessed this many times in older couples when you can still see the glimmer of a younger romance. These are the couples you hear about who die within days or weeks of each other. Their bond is so strong that when one dies, it is only logical for the other to join.

These couples have found a trust in each other that is beyond typical human relationships. They seem to be able to allow each other to spread their wings, to expand and follow their hearts without any real reasoning, only wanting their beloved to find what they are in search of, going with them willingly. The people in these relationships seem to not only have love for each other but love who they are continually becoming. The passion is in the other's happiness as well as their own.

I felt that way about Michael. Somehow, in one conversation, we shifted into one of these relationships. I could sense what he was doing, what he was feeling, and where he was. I no longer had to rely on the faith of knowing that all was well if I did not hear from him. I could now feel him as I had before we met in physical form. I could sense what his plan was.

• • •

One Sunday afternoon, I could feel that he was having a good time, and I smiled to myself. That evening we had our usual happy conversation. It was always fun to spend hours talking into the night together. I sometimes wondered if we communicated more than we would in person because the phone was our only means of being together. Although we texted almost daily, it was usually just one or two brief messages, and hearing his voice made me feel closer to him.

During the conversation, we talked about my upcoming birthday, which was the following Wednesday. Forty-four was such an amazing year for me; I hated to see it go. I wasn't fond of birthdays in the first place, as mine had a history of unpleasant memories. Somehow, year after year, my birthday shifted away from the typical celebration into a drama — often of epic proportions. One year my friend got bucked off my pony during my party, which put me in the nonfriend zone for years — not a good thing for an eight-year-old. The following year, I broke my arm at a Girl Scout party. Our leader did not believe me that my arm was broken, so I spent the entire night in painful agony, only for her to yell at me the next day for not making her aware I was in pain. I thought spending the whole night in the corner weeping with my arm cradled in my lap should have been enough of a sign for her — that and the fact I had told her it was broken seemed sufficient to me. Another year, a one-hundred-year flood ended my party early, and the next year, my aunt's death turned my birthday into a nonexistent day.

As I became an adult, the uniqueness of my birthday celebrations continued, often with evenings spent with drunken partners who inevitably spent the night telling me that I was no fun because drinking was not my area of expertise. Even if I had one or two to enjoy myself, it was not enough; occasionally when I pushed further to join the crowd, I ended the night over the sacred porcelain throne.

I learned to consider a quiet night indulging in my favorite cake with my family a success for transitioning into the abyss of aging. This year, I was expecting that kind of quiet peace, but it felt different too. I had grown and experienced so much during the year, and I was exploring a new career, one that truly resonated with who I was. Even more importantly, this year I had found the One. I met my twin flame.

I was truly happy and truly overflowing with love. I was looking forward to an exciting new life full of infinite possibilities, all of which excited me. And this deep joy radiated from every cell in my body. I could feel it. This year, my birthday was going to be different. This year was not going to be about finding my life's purpose, a new career, or my twin flame; it was going to be about me *being* all those things.

• • •

On the night of September 11, Michael called me. He sounded tired and disappointed. His day was spent with people he really liked and enjoyed, good men who were kind and loving. These men were generous with him, but he seemed very sad that these same people could be so callous and blind. All of the men he was working with were firefighters on September 11, 2001, when the twin towers came down. Every one of them lost the peace, security, and normalcy they believed would always exist. Each had welcomed a new enemy and a new threat into their lives. Their new focus held their lives together, but it also perpetuated division, hate, and anger.

Michael endured the day with them listening to their false beliefs regarding the attack. Michael himself had lost a cousin in the towers. He had also done his research and knew that there were too many untruths to come to the simple conclusion that the Muslims hated Americans and what we stand for. Yet out of respect, he listened and nodded as he felt he should on such a painful day.

As he told me about the conversations throughout the day, I knew it brought back the suffering from his own heritage. As an Irishman, he endured similar hatred and distrust against ordinary people wanting to live their lives in their own traditional ways. During the years of unrest in Northern Ireland, Michael was questioned about being a terrorist while living and working in England. He personally had felt the scrutiny, fear, and powerlessness of being from a place deemed dangerous by the powers that be. He had also felt the tide turn as the Irish became the emerald of the Queen's crown, only to be replaced by a new terrorist group, the Muslims.

Michael felt as though he didn't tell his truth to these men. He only nodded and stayed quiet throughout the day. He respected the retired firefighters for their service and the pain of the losses they suffered. Yet he felt that by saying nothing he was endorsing the hatred that was the cause of so much suffering for an undeserving group of people.

As I listened and felt his frustration with the whole situation, I told him, "It is not our place to wake people up. It is only our job to be there when they ask questions and to answer them with the truth as we understand it. You did exactly the right and perfect thing. They have been forever changed and will most likely never recover from the horror they have lived through. You can only be there to give them love and understanding, and you did that."

I understood where he was. So often with friends and family, I hear things that make me crazy. I listen as they struggle with the way things are in their lives, as if they live at the mercy of whatever is happening around them. But in reality, they have the ability to change their lives simply through their thoughts, beliefs, and feelings. This is why both of us went through the Infinite Possibilities training program. We wanted to learn how to teach people what is possible and how our thoughts really do become the things and events in our lives. Still, the basic principle of the program is that the information is only intended for those who want to change their lives and are seeking a way to do it. Michael knew as well as I did that no matter what he said, it would not have made a difference to his coworkers.

We ended our call with our usual goodbyes and expressions of hope that things were changing despite the days when we could only see sadness and pain. We knew that we were a part of the change taking place, and that was all that mattered.

• • •

The next morning my phone rang early. It was Steve wishing me a happy birthday. "Oh yes, I'm forty-five now. Thanks for the shocking news so early in the morning!" I teased him. I expected the early-morning call to be from Michael, since that's what he had promised the night before.

My phone and Facebook page were both filled with love and wishes for a wonderful day, none of which were from Michael. It didn't matter. I was having a love-filled day, and even though it was uneventful, I was happy and content that all was well in my life. The boys and I ate dinner at my parents'. I enjoyed the love my mother showed me this year; it was unlike her to give me a gushy, flowery card, but she seemed to want me to know how much she appreciated who I was. It was the perfect day, and before I went to sleep, I texted Michael and said, "Love you babes." I hadn't heard from him, but I knew everything was all right.

Two days later, I had moved way past thinking that he had phone problems again or that everything was all right. I arrived at complete indignation that I hadn't heard from him. How could he have missed my birthday? It was such a shock. Still, I was half expecting him to show up at my front door to surprise me. I contained my annoyance as best I could and tried to focus on all the love I did receive from all the other people in my life. Michael's silence left not only me but many of my friends scratching our heads as to what was going on with him — or what he possibly may have planned for me. They asked me questions like, "Did he know it was your birthday?" I assured them that indeed he did know. It was a mystery, one that I chose to leave in his hands to answer rather than speculating on it.

It was not until the next night just before midnight that his call finally came. I did not answer the phone. I did not know what I would say. He left a message: "Hi Babes. I miss you. I hope you can call me back. Talk to you soon." His speech was thick, as if he had been drinking, and he sounded a bit hesitant, although the words in his message made it seem as if everything was normal. Feeling disinclined to even deal with what to say to him, I did not return his call. He could wait until I had some idea as to how I felt about not receiving a call for days, much less him missing my birthday completely.

Trying to keep my mind occupied, I called Steve to do some manifestation and healing work. I knew it was not a good idea to be focusing on what had *not* happened rather than the possibilities of something more wonderful that could be happening. I also knew nothing was going to make me happy again until I could shift into a different mindset.

At the moment, my mind was reviewing all the past harmful and uncaring things my partners had done to me over the years and how I accepted their behaviors. This time, I was not sure how to feel. My thought was always to stay in place with an open heart and to appreciate what each individual gave me. I tried never to focus on what they had taken from me or what they didn't give me. That is, until I could no longer ignore my needs not being met, which in each case eventually caused me to leave the relationship. I did not want that this time.

I felt that it was my responsibility to be completely invested in this relationship, and that meant I needed to set my boundaries as to what was acceptable and what wasn't. It seemed that missing my birthday and not calling me for several days afterward was over my limit of acceptance and ability to think that all was well. I deserved to be cared for, regardless of the situation he may have found himself in. And based on his voicemail, it did not seem that he was in an apologetic mood. Not to mention that I called him in the morning before he should have left for work and had not received a return call until almost midnight. I gave him the benefit of the doubt and reached out to him when he was the one who should have been reaching out to me.

Working through all this with Steve helped me significantly, and I pulled together a visualization of me existing in a relationship that was loving, caring, and mutually respectful. It was a vision in which I felt I was just as much a priority in my partner's life as he was in mine. I did not visualize that partner as Michael; I just stayed in the feeling of what I wanted to experience. As if on cue, Michael beeped into the call.

My reaction was not what it should have been for someone I loved so much. "Oh crap, it's him," I said to Steve. "I don't want to talk to him."

Calmly, Steve said to me, "Kim, answer the phone. You don't have to say anything. Just listen and see what he has to say."

With a huff, I clicked over to his call. "Hi," I said flatly.

"Hi, hi, hi. How are you doing, Kimberly?" He asked in his typical uplifted way. This time I could not hear any drink in his voice.

"Well, Michael, how do you think I'm doing?" I was frustrated that he wasn't addressing his absence over the past few days.

"I don't know. You don't sound happy. Is something wrong?" He still did not sound at all like I thought he should, and I did not want to have to tell him why I wasn't happy.

He obviously wasn't going to say anything. I knew I was going to have to be the one to do it, which made me angry at myself for even answering the phone. I steadied myself so that I could remain in control. I said as calmly as I could, "Michael, I have only talked to you once in five days. Where have you been?"

"We talked yesterday, didn't we?" At least he was starting to sound a bit confused.

I was trying to keep my voice as flat and as serious as possible. "No, Michael, we talked on Tuesday. Check your phone. It's Saturday night — or I should say Sunday morning? What is today's date?"

"Well, Tuesday was the 11th, so today is the 16th. Why?" he questioned me, starting to sound unhappy too.

"Did you miss something this week, Michael?" I asked. I got no answer in return, so I continued. "It was my birthday." Still no reply. Then I felt a sinking feeling from him, and I said, "What happened? Do you have anything to say?"

"Well, yes. It is an important day for you and your family. It's the day you came into the world." His ridiculous answer only fueled my fire further.

"Really? That is all you have to say?" I asked. I was so upset that I continued with a low blow. "Remember how you told me that your father always missed your mother's birthday, and how much it used to hurt you that he didn't care enough to remember? Well, congratulations, Michael, you have officially become your father. And I am not as strong as your mother not to care. How much have you been drinking this week?" I was serious and a bit cruel, but I meant every word that came out of my mouth. I knew his father was his weakness, and I went straight for the heart because it was the truth.

"We have had a few every night, but we have been working late, and I haven't missed getting to work at seven every morning. I'm still working now. The owner is pushing hard on this last part to get the bar open soon, and I can talk to him to see if he will let me go so I can come to Florida to see you." I could tell he was reaching, trying to make amends in one form or another.

"Michael, I don't understand how you could not have called me Wednesday. Any boss in the world would let you take ten minutes to call your girlfriend on her birthday. You can't tell me that you could not have made that happen. You obviously enjoy who you are working with and have made it important enough to stay late and be early because you like it."

"And the money," he interrupted me.

"I know. It's all of it. It's a priority to you, and I need to be a priority too."

He interrupted me again. "Kimberly, are we still together?"

"Michael, you need to decide that. I am here. I have been dedicated to you since we met and before you came to Florida. You need to be the one to decide that. Do you love me? It's okay if you don't, but —" I didn't get to finish.

"No, no, I do love you," he jumped in.

"Michael, I love you. If we are to be together, then you need to find a way to love yourself enough to let yourself have everything — all of it. Your dreams, Ireland, the work you want to do, the fun you want to have, *and* a woman who loves you endlessly and completely. You have to let go of every story you and others have ever told about who you are and start writing who you choose to be in your own words through your own heart. I hope you have the strength to do that, Babes. I love you." That was it. That was all I had to say, and I said it with all of my heart.

"Kimberly, you have said some profound things, and I need to think about what you've said." He sounded just as he had when I explained how I knew I loved him.

I gave him all my heart and put it in his hands. "Michael, I love you. However, it is in your hands. I am here."

He hung up the phone telling me he loved me.

That was the very last time I ever spoke to him.

Two days later, I sent him a text message saying, "I never thought you could hurt me this bad." I never thought that he could have. I knew that how I felt was my own responsibility. Early in our relationship, we agreed that nobody could make you feel anything that you didn't want to feel and that every feeling we feel is how we choose to perceive what is happening in our lives. However, the simple fact is that I am human, and I was hurt.

CHAPTER ELEVEN

INTO THE CONTRAST

We choose to be human, to have this physical experience, to know what it is to touch, feel, taste, forget, and remember to recognize that all is well, all is divine, and all is exactly as we choose it to be. Our minds have been programmed by our egos, and our egos gauge our worthiness as physical beings. We can understand divinity and our desire for expansion by losing control over our minds, but that does not always eliminate our struggle. But if we recognize the struggle as a roadmap to our ultimate awareness, we will never become lost.

I walked around the Orlando airport passing time between my flights and looking for a place to continue writing my book. I had begun writing a journal just for my own sanity, but the pages quickly told a story that I knew needed to be written so that no other would feel alone through such a journey. I realized how often I travel alone. I traveled to the other side of the world alone when I was barely twenty years old. I gathered a few bumps and bruises along the way, but nothing truly damaging.

I am comfortable alone, but I do long for a relationship with the One I can love endlessly, the One who will always be there, growing with me and loving me. I wonder how I created this reality, one of being more at ease by myself than as two. Or was it something else I created? Was there some other lesson I needed to learn? Sitting and enjoying my glass of merlot and the first food of the day, I started writing chapter 10. Why the hell did that relationship end so abruptly, and why am I so okay with it? What am I supposed to do now? I spent years focusing on creating a relationship in which I would live happily ever after with a balanced, loving union that was full of laughter, fun, travel, and endless adventures, a relationship based in truth and honoring each other's soul purpose and the work we had come together to do. I had just barely found what I asked for, and now it was gone.

I paused to watch other travelers as they passed by. I knew each one was somehow a reflection of myself. I decided to look for some kind of pattern. Maybe if I could recognize something in them, then I could understand what was happening in me. If Michael was no longer around for me to see my reflection, maybe I was supposed to look in a bigger mirror — perhaps humanity as a whole. Feeling rather smug at the brilliance of that thought, I let my eyes wander while I opened my mind.

The general pattern in my life lately was filled with people who were very kind and nice, reaching out and offering to help me. For the first time, I was not just allowing their support, but I was hungry and grateful for the assistance. In the past when someone tried to help me, I was not very receptive. I believed that taking help was not necessary for me, being so capable and all. There was another reason too. If I accepted help from another, that would mean I would owe that person something in return. This was not just a theory for me but a learned lesson.

On the occasions when I did reach out to someone and ask for help, their response was usually unwelcome: "Sure, no problem! And in exchange, I know you won't mind watching my misbehaving motley crew of pets for two weeks while I am vacationing around the world. By the way, each one has behavioral issues, so if they snap at you, just ignore them. They also have intestinal problems, so plan on cleaning up their shit."

Yep, I learned that paying professionals and relying on my own abilities was much less taxing in the long run. Again, the concept of being on my own seemed to work for me. At least it did then, but was it still working? I really enjoyed having someone around who offered to make me tea without being concerned with what I would have to do in return. The fact that Michael would make tea just the way I liked without needing to ask me was a thrilling experience. Was I actually becoming dependent — maybe not physically dependent, but emotionally dependent? I could see how emotional dependency lingered on the edge of my consciousness. Pondering whether this was a good or bad thing became a part of my daily routine — one I did not like and that I worked to push out of my mind. But it remained there whether I liked it or not. I understood that this mind circle was created only because I did not have an answer to my problem.

Today was more of the same; my mind was set on the spin cycle. People walking past me appeared happy and helpful. As they moved through the airport, it seemed as if they were reaching out to me with their eyes, connecting with me and reassuring me with the slightest smile or nod, acknowledging that they saw me. Somehow, these random strangers came into my existence. They told me they recognized my searching. They knew I would find my answers. I laughed at myself, looking around to see whether anyone noticed. What if I am really in a funhouse full of mirrors? Was what I was seeing just a distorted reality? Were these people really smiling at me because they could tell I had completely lost my mind?

I quickly scolded myself. "If you think you are crazy, then you are crazy. Remember, you teach that thoughts become things." I consciously pushed the delete button in my mind, and then I gave it a few extra taps just to be sure the thought was gone.

• • •

I returned to my original search, looking for a pattern in the mass of humanity on the move. I began to analyze what I was seeing. All of these people and the people who were showing up in my life, both new and old, were my reflection. And if they were usually loving, helpful, and happy, then I must be as well, right? I did feel happy with my life. I knew I was helpful and loving despite my newfound freedom of saying no when I really wanted to.

Yet the doubt lingered in my mind. Was this happiness real or something I wore like clothing? I knew that we teach best what we need to learn most. I was sure that if I was actually happy and in alignment with the wonderful things in my life, if I visualized those things, then they would show up for me. For the moment, I knew I had knocked myself out of alignment with my constant repeating thoughts. Instinctively, I understood that my thoughts were adverse to my true feelings.

The only exception to the general pattern of well-being and independence I was experiencing began with my father. When he fell from that ladder, he broke all the bones in his ankle. The entire accident was a disaster from the beginning. On the way down, he knew it was going to be bad, and he was right. After the swelling subsided and the surgeon pieced together his shattered bones, he was admitted to the hospital with a gravely serious infection. That was the day I called for Michael, wanting him to be there for me.

As I was growing up, I don't recall much participation on my father's part.

However, he has been my hero and support through thick and thin during my adult life. He travels with us for all the boys' sports and comes to nearly every one of their games. Weekly, he stops by to take care of some thing or another around the house. He has been my business advisor, my friend, and my sympathetic relationship counselor. He even bothered to read a 312-page book to try to understand my point of view and build a deeper connection with me. Author David Wilcock was able to explain how I saw the world to my father though his book *The Source Field Investigations* — something I had tried to explain to him all my life with only mild success. He did it all in an effort to build a deeper, more meaningful relationship with me. The effort he made meant the world to me.

Occasionally he would need something from me, but mostly he just liked being there for the boys and me. At the time of his accident, I wondered about the timing of it all. Why did my father move into the shadows when Michael came into my life? He was happy with Michael. He knew it would take a special kind of man to be with me. He even asked me how things were going from time to time, to which I would reply, "We are both very much enjoying the unfolding of it all, and that is about all we know for sure." I knew that he understood and respected our space.

The interruption in the well-being of my family's lives after my father's fall and subsequent life-threatening infection forced me to question whether it had some importance other than his health. My father is usually very healthy, fit, and active. He doesn't get sick or hurt. His accident seemed very odd to me because of my belief that we each create our own realities. We each draw experiences into our lives to either enjoy them or learn from them. When groups of people experience an event together — an economic crisis, for example — it is usually because of an agreement between all the souls involved. My father's accident was not enjoyable and was extremely frightening, so I concluded it must be something we chose to learn from.

Did I need to create space for Michael to assume the masculine role in my life? Did my father create it so that he could learn to rely on my mother as a partner? Did he believe that Michael would be there for me forever, just as I had? I thought that Michael would always be there for me, but he wasn't. He was gone.

Strangely enough, I did not tell my parents about Michael leaving my life when it happened. At first, I wasn't even sure what happened. Eventually, I felt like I couldn't tell my father. He knew the truth that too few did: Michael was the One. Losing the partner I longed for was the biggest blow I had ever experienced in my life. When I finally told my parents what happened, the words came out of my mouth so calmly that it was almost eerie. My mother immediately put in her two cents about how nice and friendly he was, but she had issues with how much he drank — justifying why his leaving wasn't such a bad thing. But my father did something that he rarely ever does and spoke up to her: "That's enough, Janet!" And the room fell silent. We were all aware of how strange it was that I was at peace with the whole situation.

Now my father no longer had an active part in my daily life. Michael was gone with the same abruptness with which he had arrived. I was amazed by how quickly we cocreated our coming together, only for it to fall apart.

• • •

What happened next hit me like a cosmic two-by-four: Steve disappeared from my life too. He was my best buddy. He lived his life without filters or boundaries. People either loved him or ran away screaming. I just so happened to one of those people who loved him, and we became instant friends. We chatted almost daily since I took his class. We worked together, healing either his clients or friends of mine. We argued about healing philosophy and practiced envisioning the future together. If we did not like what we saw, we would work to change it using Theta practices.

One of my issues, especially after Michael disappeared, was reverting back to the old pattern of believing that people would not be there for me. Steve would treat me as his patient and would help me to envision people who would always be available to support and love me. One evening, as if we were reading straight from a school literature textbook, Steve and I experienced foreshadowing at its finest. It still makes the hair on the back of my neck stand up when I think about it.

"Now look into the future," he said, instructing me. "I want you to see that I will always be there for you."

I did as I was told, but I saw nothing. I pushed harder to focus. Still nothing. I gave up and said, "No, I am sorry. I don't see that."

At the moment, we were focused on me and the blockages that were preventing me from believing in my own worthiness. Instead, we should have been focused on Steve. Less than a week later, the FBI arrested him and accused him of killing someone in another state. He was extradited, and my vision came true. He was no longer part of my life.

My personal well-being always seemed fine and stable, but it was obvious now that something was going on in my life to create the men I loved and counted on to be taken away in a split second. Each one represented a different relationship, each radically different from the others. But I became dependent on their love and acceptance.

• • •

With time still left before my flight, I decided to get some coffee. As I stood in line at Starbucks, I realized that I missed Michael. And I missed my active, vibrant daddy, who understood everything about life. And I missed my buddy who willingly spent hours distracting me from the fact that Michael was gone. This forced me to become emotionally independent. I was going to have to learn to love myself all by myself without the validation of men in any form.

I knew the issue was solely with men. I never needed my mother or girlfriends to validate me. Instead, it was the men I chose to love that I struggled with. First, I wanted them to appreciate not just the fact that I was a woman but that I was just as capable as any man. Then I wanted them to "desire" me in the typical boy/girl way. Then, realizing that was not the part I wanted to play, I would go after men who would validate my intelligence. "Ah, excuse me, I have a brain, you know." Once men began looking at me as an overachiever, I needed them to see me as a woman.

As a result, I learned to be the perfect wife and companion, cooking, cleaning, and providing extraordinary service in the bedroom. But it was just that. I was performing services to become worthy of their attention and love. With Michael, I was looking for a hero — the only perfect one in the entire Universe. I found him. He saw me as complete. There wasn't a single thing that he wanted or needed from me.

As accepting as I was of this process of expansion, of leaving behind what was, I never once embraced the fact that I am actually human — a female human at that. Divine or not, I very much missed the physical reality of Michael. I never cried. I didn't mourn his loss, tear up his picture, or remove his contact info from my phone. I never blamed him. I didn't feel as if anything was wrong with either of us. In short, I was not acting like a normal girl. I like to think of myself as a divine aspect of God, but I am quite physically human. The disconnect came together in my mind like missing puzzle pieces that had fallen to the floor. They were just lying there, waiting for me to look down and see the connection. I realized I needed to be a human and a part of this earth, and that included contrast and sometimes pain.

As if on cue, my attention was pulled to a man who was pulling his suitcase and walking directly toward me. He had curly hair, a full beard, and a fanny pack around his waist. For a split second, I saw Michael just as I saw him walking out of the terminal in Fort Myers. When his eyes met mine, the sapphire blue I was expecting to see was not there. I was both relieved and disappointed. Tears began streaming down my face. I found my way back to my gate and took solace in the sweet warmth of my caramel latte.

I wondered why this feeling was surfacing now, in the middle of the Orlando airport. My mind should have been thinking about the business meeting happening the following day or on the book I was just beginning to write about my quest to find "the perfect one." Everything that was happening seemed totally illogical at the moment. Spock was right about us; humans use too much emotion.

• • •

I took my seat on the plane and was digging through my bag during the "turn off all electronics or we will all die" part of the preflight safety speech when I found that stupid book again — *Eat, Pray, Love*. I was starting to hate Elizabeth Gilbert. She always seemed to be able to fuck with my life just when I thought I had put it back together. When I was trying to formulate how I was going to write my book, I searched my shelves to find a book that was the perfect size, look, and feel that I wanted. The book, of course, turned out to be *Eat, Pray, Love* — very fitting, since the movie began this entire adventure of me looking for the perfect man. I recalled that I grabbed the book before leaving for the airport and added my name to the spine. It was an excellent visualization process. Fake it till you make it, right? It never occurred to me that the book would once again send me searching my soul for answers. I decided that since it prompted my personal emotional drama, maybe it was time to actually read it.

The hum of the plane's engines drowned out the neighboring passengers' conversations, and I got lost in my thoughts again. I recalled that I once chased a man across the globe. I did not love him. I was of sound mind enough to know that for a fact. He and I shared an intensity when we were in each other's presence — a fire that sparked either intense lust or the desire to kill each other, the latter usually being the winner.

When I arrived on the other side of the world on an island off the coast of Asia, I received a rather lackluster welcome from him. It wasn't the "oo, aw" kind of reception I wanted *and* actually expected. His news that he was in a relationship with the woman he would eventually one day marry came with more enthusiasm than his greeting for me had. But he had decided to let me come anyway because, as he said, "It's nice to have people from home visit." Well, good for him. At least the intensity between us was gone — and hopefully the battles. The only thing left to do was become a tourist, which I took full advantage of.

That memory brought up mixed feelings for me as a distant adventure with the pain of being used by someone. Yet the emotions from that trip felt so far away that it was an effort to pull them into my heart to really feel them. Although it was momentary, I allowed them to bubble up, to be realized and dealt with. As I released the emotions, I felt a sense of relief. I wondered whether there was more damage done on that lone journey than I had previously thought. Maybe the bumps and bruises left behind some scars that needed to be healed twenty years later.

Was I using those scars as a means of protection? Was it safer for Michael to miss my birthday, thus allowing me to deal with a more familiar, painful emotion than allow him to reject me later as I gave up my life to follow him halfway around the world? I would have followed him anywhere. I would have lived with him in a hovel if he had asked. Did I not trust myself? I knew I trusted him. I trusted him to not only protect me but to keep me safe, and I never dreamed that he would ever lie to me. There was never a reason to. I did not place any boundaries or restrictions around him that would create a need for him to protect himself with lies. Couldn't Michael just have ended our relationship, rather than just vanishing, by saying something like, "Good news! I'm back together with my beloved ex. I know how happy it makes you seeing me happy, Kimberly. Who loves you, Baby?"

"Who loves you, Baby?" This was his usual salutation, and I hated it. I think he knew it too. It came from a class assignment in which every student was required to write a letter to a famous person. Michael, never quite in step with others, surpassed the typical Irish kid enthusiasm of writing to Irish sports players and instead wrote to Telly Savalas, the famous actor whose tagline was "Who loves ya, baby?" To his delight, he received a signed photo of Mr. Savalas in return. His parents proudly framed it and hung it on his bedroom wall. That saying was one of the few things I did *not* like about him. It wasn't because he said it to other people but because I wanted my own personal endearment. I was an only child, after all.

I realized that my wandering mind could easily have created a vision of me being dumped in a magical land of bogs and ancient history, going from "Baby Face" to "thanks for visiting" in one fell swoop. Yes, missing my birthday and then disappearing into thin air was definitely the better ending than being dumped on some far-away island off the coast of Europe.

With that thought, it suddenly seemed logical that if I allowed myself to feel the devastation from the experience, if I allowed it to flow, then maybe it would release both of us, allowing us to go on with our lives. We were twin flames; what I experienced, he also felt. If I could let go of him, if I could let go of the pain and confusion, then maybe our story would become one of transformation instead of lost love. That was it! I decided that once I landed, I would find a spot on the beach and release all the pain, fear, and shame that I could muster — just like Elizabeth had in Bali.

• • •

Two days later, I arrived home and shoved that stupid book, *Eat, Pray, Love* back on the shelf, vowing to burn it one day — only to discover that "oh joy," the movie was making its television debut that weekend. While I was away, I had spent four hours on the beach trying to release the pain. Wasn't that enough? "Seriously?" came out as a whisper from my now pure heart more so than a thought in my mind, which I think, at this point, had officially quit on me. Goodbye to any remnants left of my ego.

In the following days, I did what any psychic girl would do with a quandary. I tuned in, tapped in, and began trying to feel Michael again. Some days I would think about him occasionally; others I would think about nothing but him. I wanted to know why; it was research.

After all, I was writing a book about finding the One, right? If I didn't understand what happened, then how could I truly heal and move on? If I didn't know what came next in my life after my twin flame was gone, then how could I finish the book? The book needed to include the contrast of living without him. I was determined to not have the last page of my book read, "And then she lived miserably ever after. The End." I had to find a way to get the answers I needed.

In the days following Michael's disappearance, I had asked my friend Steve to tap into him in an effort to find out how he was feeling. Steve had a remarkable gift for seeing the future, but he was clear that his purpose was to not tell fortunes. Steve also believed strongly that we are creators of our own destinies. For him, peeking into the future was more about checking on your current path rather than a psychic tool to be used to see the end result. One evening, I asked him to look for the answers to my questions. At this point, I still believed that Michael would eventually call me. As Steve meditated on it, he fell silent for a very long time, so long, in fact, that I thought he had fallen asleep. I interrupted him and said, "Well, what do you see?"

His answer was more of a question, "Are you sure Michael is as brilliant as you think he is? I really can't find anything there." Michael could be slow about some life aspects, but his brilliance showed in uncommon ways. In other words, you had to be really intelligent, both mentally and spiritually, to see how brilliant Michael actually was and how he was always a few steps ahead of everyone.

I began to wonder whether Michael had some ability to mask or cover what Steve or I could see. As a regular practice, I used white light to protect myself from unpleasant energies. Was it possible that Michael was feeling Steve's psychic intrusion and was doing something to block us? In my quest for knowledge, I pushed Steve in a different direction, away from Michael's thoughts and into my future. "Can you move through time to see if I will ever see him again?"

Loving any challenge, my devoted and supportive friend dove in. This time, however, it was only a minute before he had an answer. "It's winter — not this winter," Steve reported as the images came to him. "You are in New York. You are talking about your book — the one he is in. He will come to you. You are with another man now, one who is really handsome but kind of arrogant too. I get that Michael is a better man for you, but the guy you are with is like, 'Yeah, you're the guy she had to go through to find me.' It's like the next step has not been created yet. You haven't decided what will happen." And just that quickly, I received a glimpse of my possible future through Steve. Coming back into full consciousness, he said, "I don't know if that is good or bad, but your book will be a success."

I was very happy to hear that detail, at least. "Yeah, if I can ever get it finished. I still don't understand why he left, though. Thankfully I will be busy writing for a while." After that night, Steve was arrested, and I never got any further than what he shared with me. With him gone from my life, I was left with my own understanding.

• • •

Every psychic understands that we as humans have control and can manipulate what we see, feel, and know from our own pre-programmed stories. We all strive to be clear channels for our clients. Some are very good at it; others struggle with the words to describe what they see. As I began looking into my future, I clearly set the intention that God, angels, and my higher self would validate what I was seeing by giving me signs or by showing me a different direction. I watched for signs that would help me know that what I was seeing I was also interpreting correctly — versus what I *wanted* to see.

When you are willing to ask for and recognize signs, they show up almost instantly. I was beginning to think Michael had gone back to England. To my relief, just as I asked, I received confirmation that I was right on track from a friend on Facebook. She, like everyone else who knew Michael (or of him), was just as puzzled with his disappearance as I was. She sent me a message and asked whether I had heard from him. I told her no and that I believed he was no longer in the country. I could feel him surrounded by his friends and enjoying himself. I glanced at the clock noting the time. It would be about 12:30AM in England. She responded, "Before I asked you, I had a thought that he left the country. I was hoping he contacted you before he went."

Spending time meditating and connecting to Michael became easier as I allowed it to happen, trusting the answers. In the month following his disappearance, I decided it was time to let go and leave it in his hands. I had gotten to the point when I tuned into him, I could easily feel his emotions. I enjoyed the good ones with him, but the frustration he was also feeling was just as tangible. Sometimes, I could go into his mind and think about the possibilities of what he would say to me. Mostly he had nothing to say and no way to explain. It was almost as if he pushed a "hold" button on our relationship. It felt like it had been suspended without any thought of how to unsuspend it.

What I did know was he believed it wasn't over between us and that it would have to be dealt with eventually — but maybe not even in this lifetime. He was working on his own personal journey, putting together the pieces he needed that would finally allow him to have it all. I knew my words had meant a lot to him. He did view them as profound, just as he said. And he needed to do that in a quiet space, relying not only on himself but on the support of his family in Ireland.

He was right about us. It wasn't over. I was hoping for his blessing over the book, but that wasn't really what I was looking for. I also wanted him to know that I had achieved my dream of sharing not only my experiences but the importance of twin flame relationships with the world. I knew in my heart that he would support me. He was the one who told me that my own personal experience and point of view was the most valuable thing I had.

• • •

Calling on angels is a daily practice for me. Doreen Virtue's book *Archangels 101* is never out of my reach. Normally, I ask for help to heal my clients. I ask for help and support for my children. Basically, I ask the angels for assistance with everything on my proverbial plate. I rarely ask for help for myself. I've found that when I do, I get bombarded with distractions as if the distractions were the answers themselves. In other words, "Quit worrying about it and get busy, Kimberly." The awesome part is the distractions almost always fix the problem or issue I was facing by allowing me time and space. This time, however, I was getting the answers I was looking for, not the distractions. I was in the flow, so to speak.

Almost every morning, I talked to my girlfriend Jan on the phone while she drove to work. She began her spiritual journey at a very low point in her life when she felt as though she wanted to crawl out of her skin. That had been the same feeling I experienced when I began the serious work of my journey. Where she wanted to go, she didn't have a clue. She wanted out, and going anywhere sounded better than where she was at the time. In the next year, while desperately clinging to her new spiritual path, nothing changed for her in the physical realm. However, every new thought, feeling, and emotion shifted her to a better feeling place, and as a result, she was now feeling happy, balanced, and in tune with life.

During these chats, we would compare notes on what we were experiencing and give each other advice. We spoke from our shared professional experiences and our intuition. I loved her dearly and valued her friendship beyond measure. I was also grateful to have someone to talk to in these uncharted realms of life. One day, she asked me to do a tarot card reading for her. I did not consider myself a card reader, but I had taken a class and used them for myself over the years. I knew the cards were about the reader's intuition. So I set the intention that the cards would give me the answers that my friend was looking for. It turned out to be really fun. I hoped that I was giving her the right answers. I saw that she had some wonderful and crazy things coming in her future. We turned into two girls staying up late, gossiping about what the cards were telling us. It was relaxing and something that I missed in my life.

One day, Jan told me she read Susan Miller's monthly horoscope, which is an excellent source for detailed astrology (I have told nearly everyone I know about her monthly posts to help them learn what is coming and what to watch out for). Jan told me that her horoscope said exactly the same thing I read in her cards with the exact same timing. This reassured me that I was getting the messages right, and it gave me confidence in the validity of the messages I was receiving about Michael during my meditations. If they were right, then I had to take action and contact him. He needed to know what I was thinking and feeling about him as much as I needed to know what he was thinking and feeling.

Sitting down at my computer, I began sorting through dozens of e-card categories in an attempt to find one to send him.

"Love"? No … well, maybe.

"Thinking of you"? Possibly.

"Just dropping by"? Seems ridiculous.

"Holiday"? Hmmm … not really close enough to any holiday to pull that one off.

"Missing you." God, these e-cards were awful! They need to work on that section.

"Funny"? I'll do funny. Michael likes funny. Some of these were funny, but what was I trying to say, anyway?

I took a breath and said to myself, "Kimberly, *you know* how to do this!" I needed to dig deep into my own consciousness to figure out exactly what it was I wanted to say. The easiest way to do that was to become my own client. Skipping to the point, I asked myself, "Why do you think you need to do this, Kimberly?"

Well … I paused, not sure what the answer was. Now I understood how my clients felt when we dove into their issues. I meditated on it for a few minutes, and then the answer sprang from my subconscious: "It is the suspense. It's the lack of closure. I don't know what he is thinking, or at least I don't have verification of what I 'feel' he is thinking. When I tune into him, I feel as if he is trying to not think about me, and when he does, all he feels is a deep, profound sadness. I want him to know that I do think about him — that I love him. I also want him to know that I am not angry and I don't hate him for what he has done, or hasn't done. If he can't or won't tell me that he loves me anymore, then at least one of us will have closure, and I can move past it."

Changing roles, I asked as my advisor, "Kimberly, what if he responds? What if he calls? What will you say to him?"

"I just don't know," I answered, and an enormous wave of sadness spread through my heart and soul.

"What if he doesn't respond at all?"

"Then I can let it go," I said, liking my answer.

"Are you sure? Are you really looking for more?"

"No, I'm sure. If he doesn't respond with at least a thank you, I will know he has moved on and that he has chalked me up to a good time in America." The harshness of my own thought hurt, but it was reality.

I gave myself the same advice I would give to any of my clients: "Kimberly, all things done in love are good things."

Feeling resolute with my decision, I turned back to the computer and the e-card selections.

I found the right category: "thinking of you." The first card I clicked on had the perfect message. The message contained the ideals that both Michael and I lived by:

"A thought is something Magic
That can reach you anywhere
And today as they often are
My thoughts are there with you."

I personalized it by saying, "Some days I think of you, and some days I think of nothing but you. But every thought I have comes from the heart and is filled with nothing but love. I hope you will always be able to feel that. Kimberly."

I clicked send, and as I heard the whoosh of my email taking my words to a far-off, distant place, I felt satisfied and whole again.

Two days later, I received an email confirmation that my e-card had been opened and read. I knew at that moment that Michael and I were done for good. For the first time, I felt there was an ending instead of a future. I didn't feel hurt by it. I was sad, but the hurt was gone.

I was happy I sent him the card. I was happy that he knew how I felt about him. His lack of response told me he had nothing left to say, and that was satisfying in a way.

With closure and a clear heart, I knew how to finish my book. I also felt I could get to work on my programs I had put on hold to work with Michael. I opened the file titled "How to Manifest Your Match" and began reviewing it. It was powerful, solid, and still true. It was time to work on my own and put my ideas into action. But the question of how to live an ordinary and extraordinary life without your twin still needed to be answered before I could teach it.

I felt sure that my students would agree with me that living without your twin after meeting him or her was not ideal — at least not in the same peaceful way that I felt about it. And they would be right; it would be better if Michael and I were still together. Knowing he was my twin gave me the ability to imagine our future together living full lives. I had not yet imagined a future in which I was living alone experiencing joy and fun.

All I had was a vision of me sitting in a bookstore, thrilled that I was signing copies of my published work. I was looking forward to the time when my readers and students would share how my book resonated with them. I could feel the joy from hearing them sharing their journey and bliss of finding their twin flames. I was excited to hear how my experiences brought new insight into the mystery of twin flames.

Oddly, one vision of my future with Michael still remained. I was standing in front of the podium in a large lecture hall. I was in Europe or possibly New England sharing my story with an audience of college-aged students. As I looked to my right, Michael was watching from the side of the stage, his eyes telling me that I was doing a good job, but he was no longer physical. Somehow, the picture felt lonelier now. The sense of accomplishment was still there, but I was to enjoy it on my own.

I knew then that I would be going through much of my work alone, and I was not ready to embrace that yet. I knew in time I would. And perhaps finding appreciation would bring me more clarity and details about my new future and what was in store for me.

I was amazed that only four months ago I had clearly known what my future held. I wanted to teach, write, and wait for my twin flame. As I was teaching and writing, he came to me — just as I knew he would. Damn, I should have planned further ahead! See what happens when you don't have a big enough plan? Only Michael could pull off life without a plan. Amused with myself, I decided it was time to make one as I began to embark on a new life adventure. It was then that the phone rang, interrupting my amusement.

It was my beloved friend and card reader, Marie. I met Marie when I was only nineteen years old. If anyone could test a reader through an unpredictable life, it was me. For some reason, she always loved me, despite the quizzical look she gave the cards as she read them for me over the years. And funnily enough, she always got them right. The first question she asked in her sweet Southern voice was, "Have you heard from your man?" I decided in that moment that I was going to make a sign to wear around my neck that read, "No, I have not heard from him!" However, it would not have mattered, since she wouldn't have been able to see it anyway. I fessed up about sending Michael the e-card and his lack of response. It was a secret I could keep from most of my friends, but it was pointless to keep that information from someone who had the power to see my life through tarot cards. I did, however, leave out the detail that I now considered that chapter in my life over and done.

"Honey, don't give up on him. I know you want to, but he just doesn't know what to say to you. He will call. Give him about two to three weeks, or maybe months. Sometimes people don't respond if they can't find just the right words to say."

I rolled my eyes at the pointlessness of leaving details out of a conversation with someone who was pulling cards as I spoke. "Really, Marie? Because I don't know what would change. I think this is really done and over. What could he possibly have to say to me that he hasn't already conveyed by not responding to me at all?" I allowed my hopelessness to come through my voice. I was never very good at faking how I felt.

"He could say he loves you." My throat went dry, and her sweet voice continued. "I also see him surrounded by women who are trying to give him their opinions."

"Is it possible that he is seeing someone else?" I choked on my own words as an evil thought raced through what was now left of my nonexistent mind: "I hope she is a demanding, wicked bitch." My own thought surprised me.

"This woman could be his mother; she is an advisor to him. Does he have any sisters? It seems like these women surrounding him could be his sisters or possibly friends. See, there is the tower card." Obviously I could not see the cards, but I knew the tarot well, and the images formed in my mind. "And the lovers. There is the reconciliation card, a two of cups. Kim, I am not getting any ending cards at all. This is not over."

My head and heart were both spinning, making me feel as though I'd just stepped into a vortex that spit me out into a funhouse boxcar — the kind circuses drag from town to town collecting tickets from young children. The ride forces you to climb slanted staircases, smashing your body into tilted walls while lights flash and music blares in your ears, the "good time" coming to an end in a hall of mirrors where reflections upon reflections disorient you until you finally fall out a chute onto the ground in front of your parents.

"Wasn't that fun?" the parents ask, smiling.

Each disoriented, nauseated child answers with the obligatory, "Yeah" assuring their parents that their hard-earned money was well spent.

"Oh God, why did I answer the phone?" I thought to myself. She was right. I was not done. As much as I wanted to be, I wasn't. I began pulling my own cards at home, hoping that the results would somehow differ from my trusted card reader's. But they didn't. I also became aware that most of my friends didn't think it was over either. They often reassured me by saying, "He'll call." Their reassurances were not just attempts to make me feel better but their actual beliefs.

The stupid cardinals even began banging on my window again. When I refused to acknowledge them by going to the window as I had done in the past, the male would perform fly-bys as if he were checking that I was still alive while locked up in my office. "Yes, I see you. I don't really care whether he calls or not!" I would scream at him as he zipped by.

The truth was it didn't matter whether Michael called. I knew he was done. It was me who wasn't done yet. It was me who was stuck in the past, grieving a future with someone who no longer existed. That was really annoying. How was he able to move on when it didn't seem like I could? Several men had become interested in me shortly after Michael forgot my birthday. I even got a little excited about the possibility of seeing them, but the action needed to take that step forward was too unstable. I lost faith and trust in myself.

• • •

One evening, a friend named David set me up by asking me to come to his houseboat to help with a healing session for two of his clients. An hour into the session, David announced that I was actually there to manifest a new man, noting that the last one screwed up and left me. His clients looked at me, seemingly giving me silent condolences with a sympathetic tip of their heads. I nodded back and was pretty sure that I looked as pathetic as I felt.

As they were leaving, I readied my plan of avoidance. David waved goodbye to them and turned to look at me with his Buddha grin, but before he could say a word, I cut him off. "Let's go to Moe's," I said. "I'm starving after that, aren't you?" I knew my distraction would work. Moe's was his favorite place to eat after our Theta healing classes. I sweetened the pot by saying, "I'll buy," and then I gave him the best angelic grin I could muster.

As expected, he said, "How cool is that? Maybe we will meet the guy we are going to manifest for you." He returned my grin. "Now sit," he said, pointing at the floor. I gave in only because I was hungry and knew it was the fastest way to get to food. I took the notepad he held out for me and started my "man manifestation" list.

I began writing:

The man that exists for me is spiritual but not weird. International in his ways, brilliant but normal, easygoing, responsible, has been married before, has grown or nearly grown children. He is someone who will enjoy and love my boys and will connect with them, someone who has enough money and financial know-how to never have to worry about money. He is tall, handsome, and very capable. He doesn't think like the rest of the world; he sees things from many points of view.

I paused, thinking, and then I continued.

> *He believes there is more to the world than we will ever really see, but he doesn't worry about it. He is centered, loving, fearless, kind, gentle, strong, and a man's man. He sees his woman as his true partner and best friend but still wants to be the man in the relationship. He protects and encourages me to chase my dreams, and he will be by my side doing it with me. In each other's arms, we are at home. We communicate without words. Oh! And in bed, we are ridiculously good together. He is someone who thinks I am fabulous and would change the night into day and the day into night for me if he could — which he would know was possible because all things are possible if we believe.*

"There, that's it. Can we go to dinner now?" I said, standing up and handing David the notebook.

"That's it?" David looked disappointed.

"Yep. That's it. Oh, wait! Add in, 'Someone who won't forget my birthday.' Are we done now?"

"I want him to have a plane too," David whined as I exited the boat's cabin.

"Fine! Order up a plane or whatever. Just do it so I can eat before I kill you!" I snapped.

I devoured my food silently as I watched David go off into whatever state he does to create a person's heart's desire as I checked in with my higher self. Did I want another man in my life? I knew manifestation would not work unless I was in alignment with my spiritual, emotional, and physical selves, leaving all David's creative energy and efforts neither here nor there to me. The question really was, what was my vibrational alignment? Did I want a man in my life or not?

The answer came to me as clearly as if someone sitting next to me had yelled it into my ear: "Yes, you like being in a partnership. That is when you are at your happiest." I glanced sideways to make sure someone wasn't actually sitting next to me. No one was there, so I gave it some thought. In the past, I had liked being in relationships, but eventually they all sucked. Then I really liked being alone. Michael actually changed my mind about how it could be. I was thrilled every time I talked to him. Being with him in person was the happiest I think I ever was with someone other than my kids. I looked back at David, and I thought, "Wow, maybe I should really try again." I decided to send a benevolent request to the heavens: "To all the lightbeings in existence, please lend strength to David and his manifestation for me. I pray it will come out better and faster than I could ever expect." I had recently been reading Tom T. Moore's book, *The Gentle Way.*

In his book, he teaches about most benevolent outcomes (MBOs). The focus of requesting things in this way and then letting it go was most helpful and immediate. David then opened his eyes and began eating.

Working with David, I witnessed many things that even I thought were freaky. Believing all things were possible meant that if I thought something that happened was "Oh my God" worthy, I could guess that it was. Not more than ten minutes later, one of those "Oh my God" moments happened. A man fitting my physical "man manifestation" description walked into the restaurant. He was wearing a sailing jacket that had the name of my favorite island on the back, St. Martin. I wasn't the only person who noticed him, and before we were done eating, David snatched one of my business cards, waltzed up to the man, and gave it to him. I could have died.

I quickly hopped out of our booth and headed for the door, trying to put an end to my embarrassment. I looked back to see whether David was following me. He wasn't. Instead, I watched as he spoke with this man with very animated gestures, as if he was explaining something of great importance. It was obviously a sales pitch about me and my finer qualities. I was truly going to have to kill him.

When David was done with his work, he joined me outside. He told me how "hot guy with a boat" was completely appalled by my ex-boyfriend forgetting my birthday. He gave him all of my pertinent details, making sure he understood that I would not be fresh on the market for long and that he should make a move and call me as soon as possible. He promised that if this guy wanted to live the life of his dreams, he should take action now. My desire in that moment to disappear off the face of the planet clearly meant I was *not* in alignment with my spiritual and emotional self. I was not ready to meet a new man. Great! More work to be done. Fortunately, "hot guy with a boat" did not call, much to David's disappointment. I felt bad for him.

CHAPTER TWELVE

A NEW JOURNEY

The amazing thing about spirituality is that what we seek, we will find. It is a basic, infallible law of the Universe. The law of attraction brings forth that which we focus on. Like attracts like. I teach this. I have witnessed it all my life, and with every student who sits before me, it is verified. The question that is often asked is, "Why is this not working for me?" The simple truth is it always works. Sometimes your true desire is only found through a journey, one you must create using a new law — the law of creation. Look to the forest to find your way.

It was time for me to change my life. Dwelling in a life full of confusion was getting me nowhere. I was following what I knew to do. I was living through my heart, and it was reflected in everyone I came into contact with. But it was time to shut down my ego, the part of my mind that insisted on creating my life story. We all like stories. These stories may have been essential to helping us understand life in our past. It was the only way we had to make sense of this mystical world that we live in.

The problem is that, through the law of attraction, the stories we tell ourselves are just fueling more of the things our stories are about. If you continually tell the story of how lucky you are, the Universe will give you evidence to support that story, and your life will be filled with lucky experiences. The same applies to someone who is telling a negative or helpless story, like, "I don't know what to do." When the time comes for them to make a decision about something, they won't know what to do. Unfortunately, these stories form barriers, confining us to repeating the same old patterns that are not serving us, that are keeping us away from our dreams and our true power to create.

I understood enough about the Universe and the law of attraction to allow myself to let go of all of my old stories. Even though I was struggling to understand the world around me, the Universe would never let me down. Understanding that was enough — more than enough, actually.

I decided it was time to focus on the small glimpses of a future I did have left that somehow refused to fade. These tiny images were held in my heart. Images of books with my name on the spine, of teaching others the truth of their divinity, of traveling to beautiful places, and of the simple joy of living as my authentic self were now mere fragments of the larger vision that I once knew — the one that was replaced by those of me with Michael living life in ease and peace.

When I brought these images out to look at them once again, I began to see a clear path emerging in front of me for the first time in my life. Truthfully, it did not look all that appealing, but it was a start. When I let myself consider other paths I could follow, teaching in the corporate market or returning to advertising and marketing, I felt less at peace and more confused, as if I knew those paths were going to be harder for me to travel.

These old paths appeared in my mind like small winding trails through the forest, well worn but unfriendly. Even though I am a fan of *Alice in Wonderland*, I had the impression that if I followed one of these trails again, I would eventually fall into another rabbit hole. Obviously, that was not what I needed at this point in my life. It was far too much work without the benefit of any joy.

As I looked again at the new path, it welcomed me. I heard Michael's words come to me: "Let's start this meeting with the end in mind." What a brilliant strategy that was! Starting with the end in mind allows us to navigate our journey without getting lost in the details along the way. The end I had in mind for myself was happiness, success, confidence, love, abundance, and a career as a spiritual writer, author, and teacher.

What would happen along the trail? I wasn't sure. I did know one thing, though: I would come to know myself even more through the journey. I began to clearly hear words as if someone were reading a guidebook, illustrated with intriguing highlights and challenges along the way — if I chose to follow it, that is. One thing was for sure: I didn't want to stay where I was. I did not want to relive my past; therefore, moving forward was my only option.

As I looked closer at this path, I noticed old, disheveled, windblown trees. They looked as if they had been there for hundreds of years, knotted and heavily rooted into an unforgiving foundation of coarse, graying rocks. I knew these trees represented well-earned ancient wisdom. The grass was growing wildly in every direction. It didn't have that "greener pasture" appearance that I would have liked. However, I refused to be lured again by an enchanted ocean, vast and deep, filled with dolphins, mermaids, and a breeze promising to take me far away to a homeland that was lush and green, a place where Michael might be. I wanted to move forward and to know more about this path, so I decided to listen to my guide's reviews of my newly chosen path.

1. *Although this path is narrow and created for a solitary traveler, you will come across much help and support to make your way possible.*

Yes, I was aware it was now time to walk alone. Throughout the years of owning my agency, I was asked many times why I had a partner and why I was not the sole owner of my company. My answer was always the same: I liked working with a partner. I loved her, and we had fun together. Even though that was true, at least for half of the years, it eventually boiled down to me owning the business by myself in the end. Truthfully, in the beginning I was too damn scared to do it by myself. So I took a leap with her that I would not, or could not, have taken by myself.

Over the past several years, every business partnership I tried to build had fallen apart. Yet friend after friend would arrive to lend their talents and support to my cause. This made me realize that I needed to work alone, accepting help when it was offered. I was learning to receive.

All right! Travel alone — check! "Will always receive assistance when offered." Hmm … didn't Professor Dumbledore say that to Harry Potter?"

2. *You must find a way to help humanity if you wish to follow this path. You must share and teach the truths that are revealed to you and share the mysteries you solve.*

That sounded a bit ominous but right up my alley. "Will help and share with others" — check. Although I have loved teaching over the years, it has always been a bit frustrating being limited to other people's material. So each time I taught something, I would incorporate my own personal experiences, but I was only allowed so much freedom within a particular curriculum to do that. However, in my heart, I knew that I needed to teach what came from my own inner wisdom and experience. That was a part of the path that I could not only follow but that I was looking forward to.

3. *Although traveling alone, you will still learn and come to understand the truth about relationships.*

Thank God! This is what it has always been about for me. It is what I would preach to my staff in my office: "It's all about the relationships we make. Anyone can do great marketing." And as an agency, we had great client relationships that lasted over decades. However, for me, personal relationships were always somehow more challenging. Making them work, at least in the "happily ever after" way, seemed to continually elude me. The ironic truth was that these relationships had provoked me to come this far, and I wanted to continue forward to ultimately find the truth about love. All right, "relationships, good" — check!

4. *You will be challenged to use every skill, tool, ability, talent, and insight that you have developed along this path. You will have to push through fear, eventually coming to the understanding that there is more to these gifts than you ever realized.*

Let's see, if this path is about looking at our search for the twin flame relationship with a new perspective, then my own personal experiences with my twin had given me a wealth of knowledge and insight. Knowing that so few had even met their twins was discovery and insight in itself. I have also learned many wonderful things about the laws of the universe and how they work. I know how to create and manifest the things I want in my life and how to rely on my intuition. I have the gift and ability to speak and listen to the other side. I am a healer, and I am a lover of many. My earthly skills range from amazing mother to leader, teacher, fundraiser, delegator, and marketing and branding expert. Evidently, I am going to need every resource, skill, gift, talent, and ability that I have in order to get through this, much of which I will likely find or make up along the way. Check. (I hope I can do this.)

5. *You must be fearless and know that if you take this path, you will be transformed into someone unrecognizable to who you are today.*

Check! I am willing to become unrecognizable to the person I am today. Who

I am today is not everything I want or need to be. Sometimes I think of people as onions. Our layers are peeled away through each one of our spiritual transformations. Every lesson takes us one layer closer to our hearts. I will be happy being transformed into something unrecognizable. I pledge to embrace the changes — maybe not at the moment they occur but eventually. I laughed at myself.

6. *Once you start on this path, there is no turning back. As you journey forward, the path behind you will vanish, engulfed by your own growth.*

   P.S. If you choose to revisit a place on this path, you will have to find a different way to return other than the one you previously traveled.

Okey-dokey! That seems clear enough — no going backward and no returning to this place where I have found safety. Looking around me, I acknowledged this wonderful place where I began this dream years ago, the place where I met my twin flame and, until recently, was very happy. Funny, it wasn't looking so wonderful anymore. The long, soft grass I once loved to lie in, feeling the cool gentleness against my skin while daydreaming about a not-so-distant future, once filled with happiness, joy, play, and love, now seemed trampled, lifeless, and without promise.

As I took one last look at the place I refused to leave, the place where I held on to the littered remnants of my broken dream, holding myself back from a new possible future, I knew it was finally time to let go and move on. In fact, this new path now seemed enticing — a new adventure as well as a much needed change of scenery. The spot where I was standing seemed to become increasingly foul with the waste and anxiety in my mind.

Feeling the pull and excitement for the new future awaiting me, I kneeled down and etched a poem into the ground, finally saying goodbye to the man and the dream that I loved so dearly.

I will not live in the shadow of your memory,
For the light within has grown too strong
And dark becomes dawn.

— Kimberly Powers

I was in the contrast, stepping forth toward an unknown destination — one of great importance. It was a journey I needed to understand from this new perspective of what my truth now was.

My guide was right. Inspiration came every day as I wrote, transforming me along the way. As I poured what I knew into these pages, my mind became clear and organized. By opening my heart to share Michael with the world, I experienced the pleasure and pain that ultimately began to heal me. I found myself again. I explored the contrast of living without my twin, the One I spent my life searching for.

• • •

As I now researched more on twin flames, I discovered that the information often paralleled my own experiences. However, when I was in the midst of the "running" phase of my relationship with Michael, a phase that almost every twin couple experiences, I could not figure out what was supposed to come next. Was it acceptance? As I read other people's experiences about the phase, it almost always ended in some intense fight. However, for Michael and me, conflict was never a part of our process. So I was not positive that we would ever come back together as others had. I have since accepted the challenge to be that person to talk about what you are supposed to do after your twin leaves. How do you go on? How do you have a future? Wasn't the end destination defined as that place where finding your twin is happiness and bliss?

For me, to write and teach about the contrast when one twin runs from the other — if indeed that is what Michael did — I needed to ask the right questions and wait for the right answers. Now that I was willing to be on this journey of contrast, the answers flowed to me easily. I was ready not only to get the answers but to understand and trust them.

My first question was simple: Why is there such bliss when you are with your twin? When the answer came to me, it made perfect sense. The peace and bliss you feel when you meet your twin in physical form happens on every level — energetic, emotional, and physical. This shifting of every aspect of your being is recognizable by everyone surrounding you and your twin. My children, friends, and family could see the deeply centered togetherness Michael and I possessed as a couple. Together, we were somehow more than just two people. We were what people expected to see on the outside — a happy couple. But that deep peace and centeredness came as a result of becoming a trinity, a trinity that included God. It was the bonding of two souls who share the same frequency as God's pure light and love. My relationship with Michael allowed others to witness the presence of God in a "being" way that we have rarely experienced on Earth before. Everyone around us could feel it. Our happiness radiated from us and in return reflected back to us from our loved ones. This radiance is unique to twin flame relationships. It shines like a beacon to the world.

Digging further, I questioned why twin flames have to separate after they initially come together. I was shown that there is a time of discovery. This is the recognition moment — the "aha!" — when the twins become aware of each other's true identities. Eventually the recognition is taken over by euphoria. They each understand that the other truly *is* their match. This energy is so strong and so intense that the Universe itself is forever changed by their divine bonding.

When you are with your twin, you have nothing to hide. Your twin sees all of you. You have a mutual acceptance of each other, allowing your purest, most authentic selves to emerge the very moment you meet. This free release from all boxes, expectations, and normalcy feels almost dangerous in our world. I would have lived under a rock to be with Michael. I would have traveled the world without a thought as to our destination, how we would get there, what our purpose was for going, or even whether we had the means to go.

Twins meet when they have called for each other, consciously or unconsciously, while living their everyday lives full of responsibilities, careers, marriages, and attachments. They call because, despite the happiness they may enjoy in their lives, they recognize there is still a missing piece. They *feel* a bliss that exists just beyond them, almost as if it is calling them forward. When twins unite, the pull they feel to be together is so intense that they are willing to let everything in their lives crash down around them.

All twin flame connections add to the structure of a new energy grid of love, freedom, and living without judgment, shame, or guilt. However, leaving everything behind to be together would destroy the purpose of these cosmic relationships. In their hearts, twin flames can feel each other whether they are together or not. There is a deep sense of knowing that they belong together, and even when separated, the peace they initially found in each other's reflections remains unchanged.

Twins don't separate or "run" because they are not ready to be together; instead, they separate to prepare themselves to *live in love*. The energy on the planet is now calling these divine souls together, but the running is necessary at this point in our evolution. It allows the twins time to deal with the requirements of existing in this physical life while experiencing union on all other planes of existence. It allows them to recognize and prepare to serve their life purpose, their calling. While they are together, in the beginning they are enchanted by the bond. It is not until they separate that they are willing to go beyond their relationship to the truth of their calling: learning how to live in a union of love, of life, with themselves and all others.

In very rare instances, some twins who come together no longer bear the duties needed for practical living, though I suspect that most are like Michael and me. We live an ocean apart. We have families and responsibilities. Yet we share a calling within our souls. We are here to serve a much less selfish purpose than simply finding one another. Our time spent apart is not for us to find other people to be with but to learn how to live with balance between freedom and responsibility. Whether we come back together in this lifetime will depend on our willingness to find that balance and again move into the vibrational frequency that allows us to come together. But there is another possibility as well, the possibility we may never match again.

The contrast seems to have expanded me exponentially. I am no longer the person I was when I was with Michael. It feels now as though I am within the sacred geometric matrix of eternal expansion. The person I was, the person I had become with Michael, and the person I am becoming all merged with the reflection of him, expanding in the same way, and with every other being I come into contact with. The contrast was teaching me the truth about relationships. The infinity of love is never-ending, ever expanding.

CHAPTER THIRTEEN

FROM ONE TO ONE

What I have learned about life is that it is not a happy ending but a continuation of learning. Choosing happiness is only choosing to wear those rose-colored glasses everyone talks about. I see nothing wrong with that choice; it seems to be one of the few good choices we truly have.

I believe that the most important puzzle piece necessary to finding your twin flame is discovering the perfect vibrational alignment of your divine frequency. Your twin flame does not exist as a person. Your twin flame is a frequency or vibration that exists in the ethereal. When you have opened up to your highest self and embraced who you are, you can connect and embrace a divine twin flame frequency in your heart. This is when your twin flame can appear in physical form to reflect that energy back to you.

I discovered that once I was able to hold the frequency of pure love, someone else who could access the same frequency appeared. Adam — remember "Mr. Kundalini" from Match.com? — reached the frequency and met me for a brief moment of divine bliss. But unlike me, he was not able to "be" or maintain the frequency continuously. So we were unable to come back together. That relationship opened me to the kundalini energy flow and propelled me further on my spiritual journey learning to be divine love.

Twin flames often appear when is it time for us to experience a spiritual awakening. When Michael appeared, it was only because I was finally able to hold the frequency of divine love continuously, as he was.

I believe that it is possible to have more than one twin flame experience. The theory that there is only one true love in existence for each of us on this planet is simply not true. Hollywood portrays that if we miss this one divine love or if that person dies, then we will be forever alone. Nothing could be further from the truth. Your twin flame is eternal. You could never miss meeting the One if you are ready for him or her to appear.

Each member of your soul family who incarnates with you has the ability to find a way back to the original splitting of the twins, much like the branches of a tree all being related to the original seed. All being part of the same tree, each branch or person in your soul family could finally realize they are one with the tree and the seed. Therefore, it is entirely possible that more than one person can access your twin core energy. All parts of the tree/family could one day achieve and match your twin flame frequency and be ready to meet you in person, making twin flames as common as soul mates. We are all one.

In my deep meditative work, I have been shown two other possible ways for twin flames to come into physical existence. The first is simply what is called a "walk-in." If you are not familiar with walk-ins, these are people who are a part of your soul family but exist in the ethereal realm. They agree to switch places with another embodied soul in the same family. This allows the embodied soul to transform back into universal energy without the physical body dying. This can happen at very low periods in people's lives, like in the case of near-death experiences. The walk-in takes over the body and carries out the work for the original soul, much like a pinch hitter in baseball. That idea may sound a bit frightening, I know, but we are all truly one. When a soul is from your same family, it is able to connect to you in spirit and support you. Sometimes people are just done living and want to move on without the physical pain of dying or leaving people and responsibilities behind.

The other possibility is more scientific in nature. It comes from the idea that time is not linear as it appears to us on Earth. Time is quantum. It exists more on an organic vertical experience. Each now movement exists on different frequencies of the vertical access, giving the appearance of space and time. In this example, a soul could choose to come in at any given moment without needing to be born. Rather, the soul creates its entire life in one simultaneous moment. I have witnessed a soul who chose to come to Earth in this manner. It was miraculous to watch and as joyous as the birth of a baby.

• • •

How do you know when you have met a twin flame? You just know. You don't wonder; you know. The relationship is so unique and gives such a feeling of being at home that you undoubtedly know that you have experienced something beyond normal.

I have come to understand that when we call for our "divine love," our hearts may be ready, but our minds still think in the way of traditional relationships. Twin flame relationships are different from any other relationship. Our twins, our exact vibrational matches, are pure light in physical form. In their eyes, we feel naked. We know instantly with our hearts that this person is the One, or at least something beyond anything we have ever experienced; however, our minds cannot always interpret such a radiant light. This causes a battle between our hearts that recognize the light and our minds that have not yet learned to comprehend it.

Just as you would not expect a student who has only practiced addition and subtraction to solve a geometry or calculus problem, you cannot expect someone who has never held pure light to instantly know how to hold the vibration of divinity. We must adjust through a step-by-step process the spiritual journey, allowing our minds to understand what our hearts already know. We are introduced to people who can resonate with the vibration of our divinity for a while, allowing us to absorb the pureness of this type of love at our own pace. As our journey deepens our spiritual awareness, we too are able to hold our divine frequency with more consistency, inviting the other person to do the same and reflect the light back to us. This pattern can continue until the divine union is complete and ascension is achieved.

Some people will meet one person embodying the twin flame frequency and go back and forth together, adjusting to one another over time. Other people, including myself, have met more than one person who is of a close enough frequency to evoke the twin flame energy, thereby allowing a more gradual development by repeatedly accessing and briefly holding our twins' energy. The important thing to realize is that a twin flame is an energy, not a person. It is possible to meet more than one person who can pull through that twin flame reflection of your divine being. Each subsequent relationship grants a greater capacity to carry and hold more of a twin flame frequency. Progressively, this allows each of us to adjust our own vibrations closer and closer to that of pure love, ultimately enabling us to hold the entire frequency on our own and complete our ascension.

Through the process of learning to hold the frequency of pure light and pure love within your own heart, you will find another who also can hold that frequency. If you do meet someone who is exceptionally close to the twin flame frequency, you will align with them instantly, and both of you will be able to propel into the alignment of your twin flame energy. This can also mean the soul mate you may be married to can eventually become your twin flame as you ascend together to higher divine frequencies.

Until both parties can continually hold and be the frequency, they will not be able to remain together as twin flames. If your twin "runs" or leaves, your mind and heart will be full of questions; it is human nature, even if we accept it on a spiritual level. Doubting whether it was real or was something you made up in your mind will only prolong the separation and slow your spiritual journey. There are no false or counterfeit twins. Rather, even twins who don't stay are opportunities to experience this energy, and often, brief meetings with them will propel both twins into a deeper spiritual journey.

When twins separate after meeting, how do they move on? Do they wait? Do they suffer? Do they ask, '"Was it real?" Were they wrong? Were they not twin flames? This doubt will only serve to separate you further from the vibration of love. Trust that all is well because you are pure love incarnate. Put your mind at ease and know you are divine love. Choose to stay in the knowing, and through contrast, you will continue your journey into a love beyond all that you have seen or felt before.

For me, I have come to realize that it is possible that Michael suddenly vanished from my life because he fell out of vibrational alignment with me. I believe that for this to happen there would have needed to be such a dramatic degree of vibrational shift that we were no longer a match.

At this point, it is important to recall that the day before my birthday was September 11. Michael was working in New York in the shadow of what was left of the twin towers. His day was filled with the residual anger, agony, and suffering of the people and city that had survived that day years before. With that kind of loss, the shadow energy alone is enough to skew a person's vibrational alignment. Many of the men Michael worked with had participated in the tragedy that day as firefighters, and all had lost people they dearly loved. In addition, virtually the entire world was grieving that day, and Michael was at the epicenter of all that energy. Being in that type of low vibration for a long period of time can have a dramatic effect on a person. This is why it is true that you should be careful who you spend your time around and what you expose yourself to. Perhaps the pain he experienced or was witnessing around him caused him to change to a different frequency than mine. And if that is the case, then it is entirely possible that one day he will return to me, if he can find a way to love himself through his pain. And I know now that if anyone could do it, it would be Michael. He believed in Infinite Possibilities, after all.

However, over the year, I have felt him transition from the energetic presence he was before we met into what feels more like the collective consciousness. I am grateful for this, as I am moving forward in my expansion into the wild unknown in search of my own spiritual enlightenment. I will love him endlessly because he is the extension of the love I feel for myself. Once that kind of love has been achieved, there is love for all things just as they are.

The fact is we are human. Through our questioning and our desires, we call forth answers. We try to understand, pick up the pieces, and move forward. In doing this myself, I was finally able to let go — forever. I began treating myself in loving ways and spending more time doing the things I really enjoyed. Letting go of Michael forever afforded me the ability to not feel the loss or want to replay what happened in a constant loop in the back of my mind. Instead, it allowed me to focus on my writing or to just spend a day in play. Talking about Michael as a joyful experience instead of a tragic loss allowed me to move toward a new, expansive direction. The change in me toward loving life and appreciating everything and everyone reconnected me to the purpose I have in the world.

I have never doubted that Michael was my twin. When you know, you just know. It is pointless for me to try to make it into something else just because we are not together and possibly will never be again. Michael showed up in my life because I was ready for my twin.

What I finally found with Michael, and through his absence, was how to love the full expression of us. I don't love him or myself any less because we are not together. This is how God loves us — as a whole, whether we are connected with him or not. Twin flame love is like this; the love we have for each other is whole and complete without any expectations.

Many of the sources that speak about twin flame relationships recognize the challenge of realizing a fairy tale ending. Most will admit that a twin relationship is not necessarily the hearts-and-flowers kind of love but a deeper, more soulful, evolutionary connection. Often, these sources say that twins come from opposite polarities. There are mixed opinions as to whether the twins need to be the same sex. I believe that gender does not matter in twin flame relationships. However, there must be a balance of masculine and feminine energy within the two individuals in order for them to come together. In other words, the typical male-female role-play isn't necessarily a description of this relationship.

For me, Michael's physical masculinity and my femininity played important roles for us in coming together. However, that will not be true for everyone. I found Michael to be very physically masculine while I am very physically feminine. His essence was calm, patient, and nurturing, which are traditionally the characteristics of a feminine nature. I have more of a masculine energy as a caregiver and problem solver. I am action-oriented by nature. The balance we found together became increasingly obvious the more time we spent together.

The male-female physical balance will not be important for every twin relationship. For me, however, it was, because I needed to learn to trust a physical male presence. Having experienced power and dominance over my feminine energy and physical body, both in this and past lifetimes, it was a necessary ingredient for my healing and for forming our bond. It was essential to my spiritual growth.

Here's the deal: You *can* manifest the perfect one for you. Universal laws have created a flawless system that has existed since the beginning of time. It allows for continuing expansion that is being created by our desires. The laws of attraction, reflection, balance, allowance, growth, and love (all of which are part of the law of creation) can all be used to help you call forth your beloved twin flame. And he or she will arrive just as you ask. Your twin will be perfect in nearly every way — not in your mother's eyes or your friend's, but through the eyes of your heart. This is an unconscious knowing we all are born with. This is how we know love is blind. Love is seen and felt with an individual's heart, and no one else can see or feel the vibration that we each carry into this world. It is the vibration we connect to, to know and realize our oneness with God.

Just as my love for Michael was blind to my eyes and logic, it was more real and powerful than any other force that I have experienced in the Universe. I did not just find Michael. What I found was a divine union with God, the Universe — albeit one disguised as a search for another.

When we go in search of our twins, we find ourselves, our own beauty, and our perfection. We find that we exist as divine spiritual beings having a physical experience with all the trimmings of an imperfect human. The Bible says that God loves us and that we exist as imperfect beings. I used to argue that idea in my mind sometimes. I believe God loves us more for daring to be *out* of grace, for showing up with the original sin of disconnection. He loves us more for daring to *find* grace in this imperfect physical world. He loves us because each one of our experiences expands and contributes to All That Is. Every desire we create, through either contrast or love, expands our realities and, therefore, expands the reality of all. It is cocreation at its finest. This simple truth has been written about for centuries.

Over the period of time that I have been thinking about, researching, and writing about twin flame love, I have come to understand how and why our twins come to hold our vibrational match, but I believe a space exists beyond that as well. This is what I believe is God's space, where we as human flesh can pull through all the frequencies of the Universe, matching the exact harmony to every living thing in existence. We become one with everything.

This is what ascension is about — the recognition of our match to all creation and living as the embodiment of love. In this state, we are able to freely create the perfection of heaven on earth.

At present, I believe that humanity is shifting to see parallels in all of us, attempting to find instant connections in everyone. This is why we should never wait to love but always begin with love. As we find parallels in others, we find that we are much of the same, wanting the same things: love, compassion, joy, and peace.

When we "see" others, we are shown not only how we can help them to heal and expand but also that healing can happen within us. By healing our own hearts first, in turn, we are able to heal others.

I believe each of us can feel one another's thoughts. Maybe some people are not as ready or awake as others are to hear in this way, but it is happening with increasing regularity around the world.

If what I understand is true, the human race can begin to embrace these changes by shifting into love and bliss and moving away from worry and fears. We are the ones we have been waiting for. We have been waiting for ourselves to fall in love with us. So when we do, watch the shift that happens!

The discovery of God within us is the alchemy that sorcerers and kings have sought for eternity. It is what turns our iron will into the golden light of grace and love. And it is our twin flames who patiently wait, tending the flame of our enlightenment.

• • •

My youngest son asked me to help him with a religion assignment on the very morning I was writing this chapter. Seeing the synchronicity of life still thrills me and always will. The assignment focused on love. His teacher asked the students to question several people regarding their thoughts about love. Funnily enough, the questions gave me the answers to my own questions that I was asking at that very moment. As he asked me the questions one by one, my answers flowed without contemplation, as if I were channeling a deeper part of me that had all my answers just waiting for the questions.

What is true love?

True love is a concept that devalues the word "love," in my opinion. Love is love. Until we learn how to love as God loves and until we can in turn love ourselves the same way, we will continue to try to label what love is. In truth, we are experiencing the emotion of love in every expression we feel. Love is whole. God's love radiates from within our hearts. It shines on another and back to us, and nothing is more powerful than and as pure as love. It's all true love.

How can you tell the difference between true love and infatuation?

Infatuation is focused attention that elevates a person above love of the self. Infatuation cannot be maintained for long periods of time because it is an illusion you create that a person is beyond perfect — flawless. This will eventually lead to anger and resentment because no one can maintain that illusion; the anger is within you but reflected onto the other. True love is simply knowing the divinity within someone without anything else necessary, just as God loves us — eternally, unconditionally, and whole. Complete.

Do you believe in love at first sight?

Absolutely! Do you think God waited to see whether we were worthy of loving? Do you think a parent who has a child will wait to decide whether the child is worthy of love? It's love at first sight. The fact is we should love everyone at first sight. If you live in that heart space, you will find the whole world to be a loving place.

Love in any form is beautiful, perfect, and wonderful. It is something we should never fear. We should never withhold love and joy to protect our hearts from others because we could be hurt. Love, joy, anticipation, bliss, happiness, excitement, creativity, expression, dancing, singing, and playing resonate with the highest frequencies of universal energy. We have called forth this new energy to Earth. Through our calling of these frequencies, we also created the opportunity for twin flame reunions. So know that you are not alone in your journey to find the one your heart remembers. You are forever loved, supported, and cherished.

My first glimpse of the twin flame experience with Adam awakened me to my divinity, to the truth that within my physical body, God does exist. I am the chalice.

As for Michael, through his presence and in his absence, he awakened me to the beauty of ascension. He showed me myself and helped me awaken to how to live in love.

May you always live in love and know you are never alone.

So much love,
Kimberly

You will know you are ready to call in your twin flame when:

1. You recognize that your twin flame exists as an energy that another person can embody and not as a specific person.
2. You feel the ache of a love that is more than you have ever experienced.
3. You recognize the possibility that there is something more than the reality you see around you and that you have the ability to change it.
4. You are willing to ask the question, "What could be better than this?" and mean it with all your heart.
5. You are willing to let go of the present peace in your life to discover the answer, which may arrive in ways that could prove to be challenging.
6. You are able to see how the universe and God are in all things.
7. You understand your connection to everyone, everything, and All That Is.
8. You are willing to face your deepest, darkest shadows and fears, bring them to the light, and love them.
9. You are willing to be with another without "having" them.
10. You know all is well without any evidence telling you that it is.
11. You recognize contrast as not inherently bad but rather as helpful to us in expanding into more than we are at the moment.
12. You seek joy through serving humanity in some way.
13. You know that you are creating your own reality.
14. You recognize that what you see in others is also within you.

The End/The Now/The Beginning

AFTERWORD

Union

EIGHTEEN MONTHS LATER

What is left to do, we must do. Though the question remains, when we have broken through the edge of what is known and understood, do we fall into nothingness? Do we let our experience go to the wind, hoping that somewhere the echo of it resonates in another's heart? If indeed we are here to learn from those experiences, is it not our purpose to help one another, to love each other by wanting others to know they are not alone as they too cross over into the wonder of something more? I have often heard that teachers teach because they cannot do, but I don't believe this. I believe teachers teach because, through teaching, there is always more to learn, and this learning comes from a much deeper place than learning from another.

Standing onstage exactly one year to the day from when I met Michael, I told the audience of 240 international soon-to-be trainers about the moment I manifested speaking to them. Michael asked only moments after we met, "What will you be doing one year from now?"

I wanted to say, "Living in Ireland with you, enjoying happily ever after." Instead, I said, "I will be standing onstage telling the new trainers how I met you." And in that moment, I created a journey that I could have never foreseen. I could have never planned the highs of the love I discovered and the lows of losing someone that forever changed my life and the choices I would have to make along the way.

I did not give my audience the details of the tragic ending of my twin relationship with Michael. I did not tell them that only two months earlier I finally learned that Michael had fallen again at work and sustained a brain injury that would forever deny him the ability to hold and maintain our twin flame vibration. I did not share the anguish I experienced in realizing that he no longer remembered our connection and that I had no choice but to go on without him, our connection existing only as a memory. Instead, I focused on telling my audience that faith and the magical Universe could lead them to their own magical journeys so that they would not have to experience the same challenges and obstacles I had endured on mine.

I could feel the love from the audience. I could feel that each person wanted to know what I could share with them. When I speak, I always set the intention that everyone who hears my voice will receive the exact message that they need and want. Those who came and spoke to me after my presentation told me how they were touched, inspired, and encouraged. A few shared with me that they too had met people at the first conference they attended.

• • •

Over the months after Michael was gone, I worked very hard to follow what I thought was my life's purpose. What exactly that was, I still struggled to find. There were so many possibilities that presented themselves. I often found myself overwhelmed with how much there was to do.

I re-created my website, exposing myself in every way that scared me in the past. I developed coaching programs. I created classes, and I tried to partner with others to collaborate on projects. I learned how to speak in front of an audience with clarity and ease. I took a spiritual business class and even learned how to create videos for the work I would be doing.

I worked with teens, teaching them how to consciously create. I spoke to spiritual audiences on how to develop their messages and market to the public. I even crafted a program to cater to the business and corporate world with daily messages.

I manifested many people into my life who helped me along the way. When I wished that I could learn how to speak, Toastmasters, an educational organization that helps people improve their communication skills, presented itself. When I had the desire to become a professional speaker, a teacher appeared who was an expert in developing public speakers. This teacher had a personal interest in me, as well. I set an intention to work with a partner who would bring more to me, who would travel across the world just for me. And he did. Even better, he stood onstage with me the night before I taught the new Infinite Possibilities trainers. He told me that everyone in the audience wanted me to succeed, and he was right — not only on stage, but also in my personal life.

Still, despite all my success, I struggled to discover my life's true purpose. I also struggled with the fact that I kept manifesting perfectly wonderful men into my life but none of them came close to the one I was seeking. I decided that I would dedicate myself to loving all while doing my life's work, assuming that this would be fulfilling. But instead of a dramatic career providing financial stability, I only seemed to dabble in different projects over the next year. I did a bit of coaching here, taught a few classes there, and spoke at various engagements once in a while.

I was successfully sharing a message, just not the one I truly wanted to share — and not with the financial results I had hoped for. It was as if my life was adrift; I was floating aimlessly among a series of very interesting things. I wish I could say how wonderful and amazing it was, but the truth is, I was having a hard time. I could not clarify a meaningful, driving purpose.

I tried not to focus on money. I often reminded myself that I was supported in every way by the universe and God. I was given evidence in every moment that told me this was true, though there were many things that showed me that much was still missing. Clients began seeking me out for my coaching services, offering to pay the rates that I used to be afraid to demand, but when the time came to do their coaching, something else would stop them from moving forward. I gained a client in Europe as a "seer." They soon learned that I did, in fact, have the ability to support and navigate for them using only energy and my intuitive sight. Yet their budget wouldn't allow them to pay me in any reasonable way.

I remembered the journey I agreed to take to move away from the frozen place I had existed in at one time. The six stages I planned for myself to go through that would move me from the place I was over a year ago to a better place in the future (the guidance I received and outlined in Chapter 12, "A New Journey"). I was in a better place although not yet where I wanted to be.

When I asked my guides what I should do, they would always encourage me to finish this book. One thing after another seemed to drive me back to finishing the book. After pulling out the manuscript and reading it again, I realized that it did need to be finished and shared with the world. It was time. There were a few holes that needed to be finalized, but I realized I had completed the journey I set for myself to travel. I no longer recognized my intention to be the one seeking the One. I traveled this journey alone; it was time to share it with the world without shame or embarrassment. I used all the talents and skills I possessed, and I learned many new ones along the way.

It was that realization that gave way to the understanding that I was supposed to expand further outward rather than simply continue an internal spiritual journey. Further, the purpose of this outward expansion was not for me to do anything other than participate in the world using my talents, gifts, love, and knowledge in any way that presented itself. My spiritual teacher often reminded me, "Kimberly, you are in this world, not of it." Perhaps after all these years and the long journey, my real purpose was to finally become "*of* this world" rather than merely surviving in it.

Not many people on this Earth are living in divine union with All That Is. It is a concept that we all seek, whether we are conscious of it or not. The reality of living it, much less realizing it, is what challenges us most. A teacher told me long ago that there would be but a few who could understand and relate to what I was going to experience. I always disagreed with this idea because I knew it was possible for everyone to ascend into love and truth. I have never let go of that knowledge and belief in humanity.

I entered this lifetime knowing that it is our deepest desire to find union with the One once again. What I learned was that this yearning, this calling, was not about finding the One but rather becoming one with all there is. It is not a mistake that we are here in this time and space. We have all decided to become human during this transition of epic proportions. Everyone on this planet came to witness the evolution from the physical human form into God. Everyone is playing some kind of role to bring about this reality.

During the Infinite Possibilities "Train the Trainer" Conference in Boston in 2013, I witnessed the beginning of this new reality. The real shift happened as I was writing to a friend I planned to share a room with at the conference. I was pondering skipping the conference altogether, mostly because of money but also because I was hoping to have a job by then. I was unsure of the purpose of my presence at the conference. Then one day I heard these words float into my mind: "Offer to do regression sessions." I have done these sessions over the years but never publicly marketed them. Always trusting my guidance, I ran the possibility of offering these sessions by another trainer. In an instant, she expressed her support and wanted one for herself. Within one day, I had nine people who were interested. It was settled. I was going to Boston, and I had manifested enough money to cover the cost of the trip.

Just a week before the conference, I was asked to do a roundtable discussion for new trainers. I was happy to do it and easily put together a session on experiments that would prove that the Universe was hearing people's thoughts and responding to them. I could feel the momentum building as I prepared for Boston. All the indecision I had experienced before was taken away, and I saw a new purpose in my presence at the conference.

I never expected to be so transformed when I went to the conference. Each one I attended before was remarkable, but this one was different. The past-life regression sessions, which I had done so many times before, took on a very different form. As I took people into the deep meditative state necessary to connect to their past lives, they began to connect to something else, something very unique. They were not going back to past experiences; each one was connecting to a higher power. I had altered my protocol a bit before I started the sessions this time, hoping to ensure my clients would achieve a very deep state of meditation, but it was not the protocol that changed the sessions. The energy available on the planet had shifted and so had our access to the divine. I asked each of my clients to breathe in the pure light of creation, something I had recently introduced into my own meditations. Then I asked them to fill every cell of their being with this light in the purest and highest vibration. I then asked them to relax as the light washed down their bodies, finally joining with the light that was radiating from within them.

As each person did this, the session brought joy beyond imagination. Many tears flowed as they witnessed "all is well" joy and love beyond their normal understanding. Each person was released from a burden of worry and invited to live life with ease and grace. In one way or another, they all connected to a higher vibration of existence than simply that of a being on Earth. Some people were invited to play with their guides, others could see angels, and still others witnessed the places where their souls were born. All of them seemed to find an understanding of purpose. Their experiences became life altering and opened them to a continuous connection to their highest energetic selves. Through the sessions, I found my purpose, the one thing I am here for, the one thing I always knew was possible: assisting others in finding a pathway to living as humans in divine union with All That Is, God. My purpose was to write and teach the law of creation — how to *live in love and consciously* create as our creator selves. It was that simple. Just as I knew Michael was my twin flame the moment I met him, I knew this was finally the purpose I had been searching for.

During the last night of the conference, another transformation took place.

I found an editor and publisher for my book, this book that I finally completed. I knew I would find someone at the conference, much like I expected to meet Michael. I connected with a trainer from Utah whom I had only really known through the Infinite Possibilities Facebook page. She had published her own e-book a year before and was encouraging other trainers to write and share their messages. It was her experience in publishing her own and others' books, as well as the fact that we shared kindred core beliefs, that convinced me she would be the one to help me bring my dream to reality. Within days of returning home, I sent her the manuscript file.

Over the next few weeks, I became aware that every conversation I was having seemed to focus on spirituality in one way or another. The new reality I experienced in Boston was now showing up daily and in many unexpected places. I was constantly engaged in open discussions about my connection to nonphysical beings. I was frequently asked how I could sense things and how my role as a seer could contribute to the companies I worked for. I was energetically helping people every day, and those I helped were spreading it to their friends. These are not things I freely talked about in my day-to-day life before, yet they were showing up in my daily life now.

People began sharing their stories and experiences and those of others they knew who had experienced things on the other side. I was someone tangible with whom they felt comfortable and safe asking whether their experiences were true and, if so, what that meant. They wanted to understand why they would see repeating numbers all around them and why they would wake up at the exact same time every night. They wanted assurance that what they were experiencing did not make them crazy. I loved that I had the pleasure of telling them it was real and that no, they were not crazy. I recommended books and websites to them and shared insights that gave them an enlightened understanding about the awakening they were experiencing. At last, I understood what I had always been searching for — my purpose: to teach what I have always known, how to connect and be in union with your creator consciousness — and the world was yielding to me.

My answer had been in front of me all along, but I was simply not yet able to see it. I spent years trying to do and find my work, even though I had been told to first seek joy and then all else would follow. In my search, I could not see what I was looking for, because what we are really searching for can only be seen through and with love, through the heart. I found love by creating an intention to understand and experience it in its whole truth. By letting go and opening up to love, I found joy. So the joy reflected back at me, and the reflection revealed my true calling.

Living with purpose puts you into alignment with everything that brings you joy, bliss, and happiness. You will know what your purpose is if you look for the thing that allows you to relieve what gives you your greatest torment. It will move you from servitude to service of humanity. For me, it was knowing the truth that all people could live in union and create anything but they just didn't know how. But first I had to experience what divine love was and pass through the eye of the needle. I then needed to experience the loss of my twin flame to understand the completeness of love, with and without, to find the ultimate union of one.

We all have something that hurts inside our hearts. When you are willing to answer the call to understand the pain, you too will find your way home and fulfill your purpose.

So what is left, then? Living, loving, being, and doing? The answer is simple: anything that is in alignment with what feels good to you. Just merely hold the intention to understand your purpose, allow the journey to unfold before you, and trust.

You will always have help along the way. Our soul mates teach us lessons; our twin flames propel us forward to love ourselves into the union of One. It is only then that we complete our journey, recognizing that we are our own heroes, living as one, that we can open ourselves to live, be, and experience our intended purpose. We then are able to experience bliss and serve in love and joy in all things we do.

If you are seeking your twin flame, I know your path will not be an easy one. You will find crevasses in your soul that you never expected were hiding buried truths. You will have struggles and be misdirected. You will awaken and marvel in the wonder and simplicity of a raindrop. You will witness what others don't bother to look up and see. Birds will speak to you, and the clouds will appear to dance for only you. You will discover that the world is not what it seems. Movies will no longer just be for enjoyment but will hold truths for those who know the message is for them. You will be guided. You will be misled. You will second-, third-, and fourth-guess yourself, until you stumble across what you know to be your truth, and it will be unlike anyone else's.

Know, however, that if you seek this path, you will be forever changed for the better. You will eventually, after a long and arduous yet *joyful* journey, discover that not only are you a twin flame on Earth and in the heavens but you also possess a light within that you will find shining back at you from within the mirror that the Universe holds before you.

As with all things, a single destination does not exist. Once you think you have arrived, another path will open itself to you. When you think you have found "you," you will expand again, and when you have expanded into union, you will find "you" all over again.

To a never-ending, ever-expanding journey of love and connection, walk forward, brave heart. Your self is waiting for you.

A NOTE FROM THE EDITOR

APRIL JOY RAIN

It is an incredible honor to be a part of this book. I want to share an extraordinary experience that happened as a result of it. In chapter 8, Kimberly tells a wonderful story about her grandfather who passed away yet is a constant guiding presence in her life. Since his passing, he has developed quite a reputation for providing members of Kimberly's family with a feather upon request. He has been, shall I say, very consistent. One night, it was very late and I had been editing the book for some time. I read that part of the chapter, and I am embarrassed to say that I asked him for one. I should have considered what I did, but I said it before I had a chance to really consider that it might be disrespectful in some way.

The following day, I resumed editing and worked for several hours while sitting at my desk. I suddenly had this sensation that felt like two of my fingers were sticking together. I wiggled them without looking down. But as the sensation got worse, I looked at my hand, and there between my fingers was a little white feather. I was astounded, to say the least. As I held that little feather between my fingers, I began to cry for the beautiful gift I had just received.

The really amazing part is I don't own a single feather item in my home. No pillows, no comforters — nothing. There was nowhere for this little feather to come from. In addition, I had been in the same location for several hours, which meant it literally had to fall onto my hand from above. Pretty cool, right?

The experience was so remarkable that it won out over my embarrassment about asking for one in the first place, and with Kimberly's permission, I shared my experience on Facebook. What happened after that was nothing short of a miracle. It is a gift that we are giving to you. We have included below the comments that followed my story on Facebook, and perhaps if you ask Kimberly's grandfather, he will deliver a feather to let you know that he hears you and that you are loved and always will be.

Following are the subsequent responses to my post on Facebook when I shared my feather story.

- April! Funny, after reading this on Sunday I thought, "Oh, that is so cool! I want to find a feather." I just found one! I was putting something on top of the fridge while cleaning the kitchen and a feather fell as if from the sky. Lovely happy moment on a challenging day. Love to you, beautiful one.
- I wanted to share that a white feather appeared into my world today, and I am so certain it is from Kimberly's Grandfather! Anyway, really cool stuff. I am grateful and happy that I receive these lovely signs from the other side.
- By the way, there was a white feather in my lap today. I don't recall actively asking for it, but I love the wave from Kimberly's grandfather and the Universe!
- So April, I read this earlier and thought how cool … then I got up to go upstairs a little bit ago and there on the second step up was a little white feather … I would normally pay no attention but I just burst out laughing!
- I thought, why not ask Kim's grandfather too! Opened my eyes to find one in front of me! That was an hour ago, I'm telling the story to a friend in a cafe and when I say I wanted to see a feather too, I see one on his arm …
- Ok, so the past week I have been really struggling to keep my happy awesome feeling going in the face of my day-to-day life. I went to bed last night thinking that in the morning I had to make some changes to get my mojo back. I decided to get out my yoga mat while the coffee was brewing. As I hung upside down in downward dog, I looked behind me and there on the floor was a small white feather. I immediately thought of your posts! Thank you to Kimberly's grandfather and to the Universe for the sign I needed to get my ass back in gear! And thank you for sharing this story!

A Note from Kimberly

My grandfather adored me and always made me feel very loved. I was fortunate to be with him when he transitioned at the age of ninety-three. I did not feel the loss of his presence but rather his full presence when I said goodbye. It has been amazing to be in continuous union with his love ever since. The first feather he gave me was on the morning when he left us. After that, whenever someone in my family thought of him, they would receive a feather.

When I read about so many people receiving feathers around the world, I realized that this simple request to Grandad has power — the power to bring awareness to the kind of love that is eternal. Ask and watch, as you too will receive a message from the other side that you are heard, you are loved, and you are not alone. They are never too busy to show you how much you are loved. My grandfather's name is John. He is waiting for you to ask, just as every angel, every guide, and your twin flames are.

Sending you so much love.

ABOUT THE AUTHOR

KIMBERLY E. POWERS is a spiritual writer, author, and teacher on the subject of conscious creation. Her passion is awakening others to their divinity. Kimberly first accomplished this mission through her international award-winning branding and advertising agency that she led for seventeen years. Realizing it was time to answer her own calling, she embarked on a spiritual journey. She found her answers one by one, finally recognizing the truth of the quest on which she had embarked: Love is Infinite.

Kimberly is a lifelong intuitive — clairaudient, clairsentient, and claircognizant. She channels angels and guides, and she is a certified Theta healer and a certified Infinite Possibilities trainer and trailblazer. Through the gifts, tools, and knowledge she has received in her life, she has found a way to embody true love, peace, happiness, and personal empowerment and share it with others.

Falling in Union, is about her real-life hero's journey to understand the nature of true love, soul mates, twin flames, and the union into one. Kimberly lives in Fort Myers, Florida, with her two beloved sons and is currently working on a second book, *ReUnion: Remembering Your Creative Consciousness through the Law of Creation*. Visit Kimberly at InsightontheWeb.com to follow her blog, read excerpts from her new book, or book a session.

OUT-OF-BODY EXPERIENCES

by Gene Schmitz

WITH CHANNELED EXPLANATIONS AND COMMENTARY THROUGH Robert Shapiro

This book not only tells the full story of Gene's life, but it also includes a detailed conversation with an angelic being who speaks through superchannel Robert Shapiro to reveal the meaning behind Gene's out-of-body experiences and his life's purpose. In the process of explaining the twists and turns of Gene's life, this angelic being also unveils some surprising truths about the connection between the body and the soul that apply to all of us.

$14.95 Plus Shipping

ISBN 978-1-891824-95-1
Softcover • 144 PP.
6 X 9 Perfect Bound

CHAPTERS INCLUDE:

- Soul Travel Begins
- Soul Travel Continues
- The White Light
- Floating Farther from Home
- My Soul Travels Resume
- Message from Grandpa
- Angels and Animals
- New Traveling Companions
- Soul Crossings

Hearing the Angels Sing:

A True Story of Angelic Assistance

by Peter Sterling

Hearing the Angel's Sing chronicles my extraordinary journeys into the higher dimensions of light where I met the angels who ultimately brought me to the realization that my mission was to be a channel for God's heavenly music. The book includes never-before-shared details of my journey of awakening. From the snowcapped peaks of the Rocky Mountains to the tropical jungles of the Mayan temple lands, the red rock towers of Sedona, and ultimately to the Incan highlands of Peru, this is a captivating story that will take you on an amazing journey of discovery!

— Peter Sterling

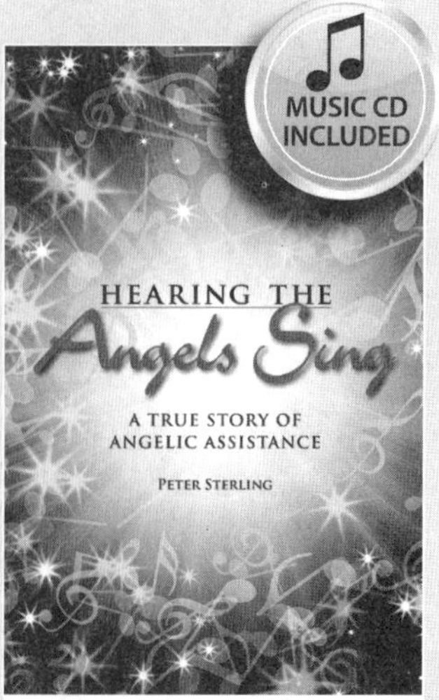

$16.95 Plus Shipping

ISBN 13: 978-1-891824-96-8
Softcover • 256 PP.
6 X 9 Perfect Bound

CHAPTERS INCLUDE:

- Descension and Birth
- Down the Rabbit Hole
- Windows to Heaven
- Rocky Mountain High
- Angels and Devils
- Harmonic Converging
- Red Rocks Calling
- To Hear the Angels Sing
- Fires of Purification

Hilary Jamron

We all have reasons for doing the things we do.

We all have our own realities. It is my blessing to have more than one.

— Hilary Jamron

$16.95 • Softcover • 304 pp.
978-1-62233-014-0

Surrealistic TRIALS

When Hilary died, part of her soul refused to come back. That part of her higher self chose to remain where peace and simplicity reign. From that time forward, life would reveal itself in front of her, and she would simply step into her future. Decisions would be made without fear or hesitation by an unconscious multidimensional consensus, and she would survive. She would travel through death and paralysis without self-pity or delay.

The truth is that each of us is as limitless as space and time, having no boundaries, beginnings, or endings. Limits are illusions, delusions, like pebbles that we casually kick out of our way as we move forward. Illness, pain, heartbreak, and life circumstances are all pebbles. There's no point in looking back when we've already kicked our earthly problems off to the side of the road. The kicking is a gentle toss of the foot done in perfect synchronicity to the drumbeat of lessons learned. After that, the only direction is forward.

RAE CHANDRAN

$19.95 • Softcover • 384 PP.
978-1-62233-013-3

DNA of the Spirit, Vol. 1

Channeled through Rae Chandran with Robert Mason Pollock

The etheric strands of your DNA are the information library of your soul. They contain the complete history of you, lifetime after lifetime; a record of the attitudes, karma, and emotional predispositions you brought into this lifetime; and a blueprint, or lesson plan, for your self-improvement. Your DNA is also a record of your existence from the moment of your creation as a starbeing to your present incarnation. This information is written in every cell of your body.

CHAPTERS INCLUDE:

- Mudras for Activating the Twelve Layers of DNA
- The Awakening of Crystalline Consciousness
- Auspicious Times for Awakening Consciousness
- Angelic Support for DNA Activation

32 color pages of mudras and images to activate your 12 levels of DNA

DNA of the Spirit, Vol. 2

Channeled through Rae Chandran with Robert Mason Pollock

This companion book to *DNA of the Spirit, Vol. 1* originated with the intention and desire to bring forth understanding to support humanity. Go through this volume while holding a sacredness inside of you, asking that the material be imprinted in your sacredness so that it may become an experience that you will be able to live.

Some of the material in this book is coded, and sincere students will find they can open these codes. Understanding can be received through your own filter and in your own way. This way, you will find the Divine within.

CHAPTERS INCLUDE:

- Auric Imprinting Technique for Healing
- The Number of God
- Reveal Your Life Contracts
- Re-create Your Life with Your Akashic Records
- Humans Are Creators in Training

$16.95 • Softcover • 192 PP.
978-1-62233-027-0

Light Technology PUBLISHING Presents

TINA LOUISE SPALDING

GREAT MINDS SPEAK TO YOU

"Many in spirit look on these times of difficulty, abundance, trouble, and innovation and wish to share with you their experiences and ideas. Some famous names and faces will come to mind as you read this book, and you will glean some fine information about their own learning, their own suffering, and indeed their own experience in the life after this life, for they all wish to tell you that there is no death as you perceive it to be. They are all there in their astral forms, enjoying their continued growth, their continued expansion, and their continued joy in living."

— Ananda

Chapters Include:

- Albert Einstein
- Jerry Garcia
- Marilyn Monroe
- John Huston
- Amy Winehouse
- Princess Diana
- Elizabeth Taylor
- John and Robert Kennedy
- Michael Jackson
- Cecil B. DeMille
- Pablo Picasso
- Queen Mother Elizabeth
- George Bernard Shaw
- John Lennon
- Jesus Christ

$19.95 Softcover, 192 PP.
ISBN 978-1-62233-010-2

CD of Live Channelings Included!

MAKING LOVE TO GOD
THE PATH TO DIVINE SEX

"We are here to teach the way to divine bliss, and we know you are scared — scared to lie naked caressing your lover with rapt attention and honor. Give love all day, and you will be guaranteed to receive love all night. The divine sexual experience connects you, God, and your lover — if you have one — together in a dance of divine bliss."

— Ananda

Topics Include:

- How We Came to Misunderstand Sexual Energy
- Using Divine Sex Energy
- Specific Steps and Sensations
- Blocks to Transformation
- A Transformed View of Sex and Sexual Energy
- Following the Path to Transformation
- Reaping the Harvest

$19.95 Softcover, 416 PP.
ISBN 978-1-62233-009-6

Print Books: Visit Our Online Bookstore www.LightTechnology.com
eBooks Available on Amazon, Apple iTunes, Google Play, and Barnes & Noble

Light Technology PUBLISHING **Presents**

THE ANCIENT SECRET OF THE FLOWER OF LIFE, VOLUME 1

Once, all life in the universe knew the Flower of Life as the creation pattern, the geometrical design leading us into and out of physical existence. Then from a very high state of consciousness, we fell into darkness, the secret hidden for thousands of years, encoded in the cells of all life.

Now, we are rising from the darkness, and a new dawn is streaming through the windows of perception. This book is one of those windows. Drunvalo Melchizedek presents in text and graphics the Flower of Life workshop, illuminating the mysteries of how we came to be.

Sacred geometry is the form beneath our being and points to a divine order in our reality. We can follow that order from the invisible atom to the infinite stars, finding ourselves at each step. The information here is one path, but between the lines and drawings lie the feminine gems of intuitive understanding.

You may see them sparkle around some of these provocative ideas:

- Remembering our ancient past
- The secret of the Flower unfolds
- The darker side of our present/past
- The geometries of the human body
- The significance of shape and structure

$25.00 Softcover, 240 pp.
ISBN 978-1-891824-17-3

Drunvalo Melchizedek's life experience reads like an encyclopedia of breakthroughs in human endeavor. He studied physics and art at the University of California at Berkeley, but he feels that his most important education came after college. In the past twenty-five years, he has studied with over seventy teachers from all belief systems and religious understandings. For some time now, he has been bringing his vision to the world through the Flower of Life program and the Mer-Ka-Ba meditation. This teaching encompasses every area of human understanding, explores the development of humankind from ancient civilizations to the present time, and offers clarity regarding the world's state of consciousness and what is needed for a smooth and easy transition into the twenty-first century.

Print Books: Visit Our Online Bookstore www.LightTechnology.com
eBooks Available on Amazon, Apple iTunes, Google Play, and Barnes & Noble

Light Technology PUBLISHING Presents

THE ANCIENT SECRET OF THE FLOWER OF LIFE, VOLUME 2

The sacred Flower of Life pattern, the primary geometric generator of all physical form, is explored in even more depth in this volume, the second half of the famed Flower of Life workshop. The proportions of the human body; the nuances of human consciousness; the sizes and distances of the stars, planets, and moons; and even the creations of humankind are all shown to reflect their origins in this beautiful and divine image. Through an intricate and detailed geometrical mapping, Drunvalo Melchizedek shows how the seemingly simple design of the Flower of Life contains the genesis of our entire third-dimensional existence.

From the pyramids and mysteries of Egypt to the new race of Indigo children, Drunvalo presents the sacred geometries of the reality and the subtle energies that shape our world. We are led through a divinely inspired labyrinth of science and stories, logic and coincidence, on a path of remembering where we come from and the wonder and magic of who we are.

Finally, for the first time in print, Drunvalo shares the instructions for the Mer-Ka-Ba meditation, step-by-step techniques for the re-creation of the energy field of the evolved human, which is the key to ascension and the next dimensional world. If done from love, this ancient process of breathing prana opens up for us a world of tantalizing possibility in this dimension, from protective powers to the healing of oneself, of others, and even of the planet.

Topics Include:

- The Unfolding of the Third Informational System
- Whispers from Our Ancient Heritage
- Unveiling the Mer-Ka-Ba Meditation
- Using Your Mer-Ka-Ba
- Connecting to the Levels of Self
- Two Cosmic Experiments
- What We May Expect in the Forthcoming Dimensional Shift

$25.00 Softcover, 272 PP.
ISBN 978-1-891824-21-0

through Elliott Eli Jackson

$16.95 • Softcover 288 pp.
6 X 9 Perfect Bound
ISBN 978-1-891824-71-5

The Sapiential Discourses: Universal Wisdom

Volume I

"*The Sapiential Discourses* contains ancient wisdom known to people since the beginning of time and new wisdoms for the new millennia. This book is designed to assist all who read these truths in their remembrance process, the remembrance of our divinity. The true natures of twin flames and soul mates are revealed. New information on the paranormal, faith, God, and parenting is included, along with other important topics that are relevant to our existence and obtaining a clean, peaceful Earth."

– Elliott Eli Jackson

The Sapiential Discourses: Universal Wisdom

Volume II

As with the first book in this series, we are given information to assist us in remembering vital universal truths as we enter a new era in human history. The book begins with the spiritual revolution that is occurring on planet Earth now. It ends with the world of tomorrow and what the future brings for us all. In between, we are given new information about signs and symbols, energy vortexes and portals, Indigos and starseeds, other planes of existence, and God and science.

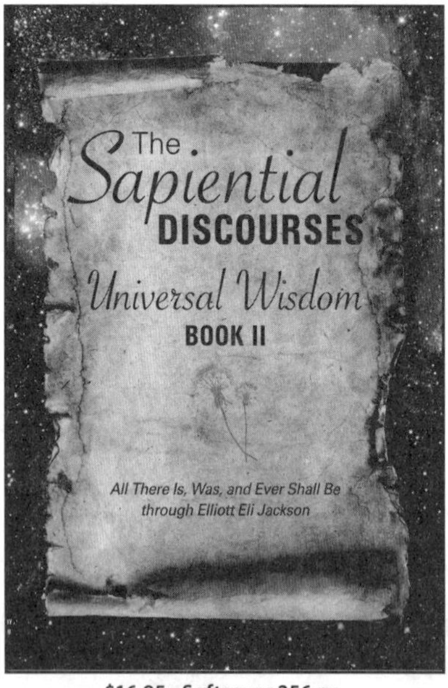

$16.95 • Softcover 256 pp.
6 X 9 Perfect Bound
ISBN 978-1-62233-018-8

Light Technology PUBLISHING Presents

$16.95
Plus Shipping

ISBN 13: 978-1-62233-017-1
Softcover 256 PP.
6 X 9 Perfect Bound

The Comprehension of the Holy Spirit within the Human Condition

Spirit of Space with Gabriel et al. through Arthur Fanning

TOPICS INCLUDE:

- The force of the Holy Spirit is coming: Are you ready?
- The forty-nine personalities in your chakras are unifying.
- Your soul force is expanding.
- Your birth name and birth date are vitally important.
- Your bones are becoming more fluid.
- The Moon rules the water in your body.
- Gratitude, appreciation, and prayer are essential now.
- Your thoughts: Are they yours or someone else's?
- All religions have the same god, the same idea, why fight?

And much, much more.

COMING SOON

Permission to Ascend

Spirit of Space with Gabriel et al. through Arthur Fanning

Light Technology PUBLISHING Presents

by Cheryl Gaer Barlow

Angels Explain Death and Prayer

"We are the angels of the Mallbon. We are meant to tell those of Earth that the death of the body is never to be feared. We help in ways not understood by humanity. We can manifest anything we desire. We can live as humans on Earth. When we absorb the reality of Earth, we work God's wonders in ordinary ways.

"When the surroundings are not in focus or when you feel unable to cope with the people or circumstances around you, be still and ask God for help. God will respond to requests of help by mending emotions with aid from the angels. This is done by being aware of the angels. We surround you and bring you comfort.

"You must, as a human race, lift the quality of thought to the highest level. When the level of thought is low and miserable, it is generated through the entire world. When it is lifted to a level of joy, it lifts all minds. When you know the teachings of the angels, no ignorance will be left in the soul. You will no longer be afraid or in pain. Now is the time to stand with the angels of God and help humankind."

— The Angels of the Mallbon

$16.95 Plus Shipping

ISBN 13: 978-1-62233-008-9
Softcover • 224 PP.
6 X 9 Perfect Bound

Angels Explain God and the New Spirituality

$16.95 Plus Shipping

ISBN 978-1-62233-023-2
Softcover 176 PP.
6 X 9 Perfect Bound

The message of this book is to tell the souls of Earth about the wonders of God, the glorious angels, the heavens, the Earth, and all existence. Know above all things that God loves you more than any words can express.

God is always with you. He is ever bringing you toward the blossoming of your soul. God communicates by way of the holy angels of God. The most important words we want to tell you are these: Open your soul. Surrender your soul to God. Ask God to lead you to truth, love, and peacefulness. Ask God for any attributes you wish to acquire. God's angels will help you become the strong, powerful soul that you are meant to become.

A world of souls, lifting their minds to reach God will affect the universe. Be the soul you are meant to be. The most powerful attribute a soul may attain is love.

— The Angels of the Mallbon

Print Books: Visit Our Online Bookstore www.LightTechnology.com
eBooks Available on Amazon, Apple iTunes, Google Play, and Barnes & Noble

Light Technology PUBLISHING **Presents**

THE BOOK OF transformation

THROUGH ROBERT SHAPIRO

Topics Include:

- Heart Heat • Safety Exercises • Benevolent Magic • Living Prayer • Disentanglement • Deep Disentanglement • Disengagement & Engagement • Connections • and much more!

— Learn how to ask for clearing of old traumas and discomforts.

— Learn how to create a nourishing, benevolent life for yourself and others.

eBook **ONLY** $2.99

with CD

$25.00 Plus Shipping

ISBN 13: 978-1-891824-42-5
Softcover 448 PP.
6 X 9 Perfect Bound

Shifting Frequencies

Sounds for Vibratory Activation

by Jonathan Goldman

For the first time, Healing Sounds pioneer Jonathan Goldman tells us about shifting frequencies — how to use sound and other modalities to change vibrational patterns for both personal and planetary healing and transformation. Through his consciousness connection to Shamael, angel of sound, Jonathan shares his extraordinary scientific and spiritual knowledge and insights, providing information, instructions, and techniques on using sound, light, color, visualization, and sacred geometry to experience shifting frequencies. The material in this book is both timely and vital for health and spiritual evolution.

Chapters Include:

- Sound Currents: Frequency and Intent
- Vibratory Resonance
- Vocalization, Visualization, and a Tonal Language
- The Harmonics of Sound
- Vocal Harmonics and Listening
- Energy Fields

In this book, you will:

- explore the use of sound in ways you never imagined for healing and transformation
- discover harmonics as a key to opening to higher levels of consciousness
- learn about the angel chakra and what sounds may be used to activate this new energy center
- find out how to transmute imbalanced vibrations using your own sounds
- experience the secrets of crystal singing

Phone: 928-526-1345 or 1-800-450-0985 • Fax: 928-714-1132

Light Technology PUBLISHING Presents

DAVID K. MILLER

FIFTH-DIMENSIONAL SOUL PSYCHOLOGY

The basic essence of soul psychology rests with the idea that the soul is evolving and that part of this evolution is occurring through incarnations in the third dimension. Now, to even speak about the soul evolving is perhaps a controversial subject because we know that the soul is eternal. We know that the soul has been in existence for infinity, and we know that the soul is perfect. So why would the soul have to evolve?

The answer to this question is complex, and we may not be able to totally answer it using third-dimensional terminology. But it is an important question to answer, because the nature of soul evolution is inherently connected to your experiences in the third dimension. The soul, in completing its evolutionary journey, needs these experiences in the third dimension, and it needs to complete the lessons here.

—Vywamus

$16.95 • Softcover • 288 PP. • 6 X 9 Perfect Bound • ISBN 978-1-62233-016-4

OTHER BOOKS BY DAVID K. MILLER

1 

2 

3 

4 

5 

6 

7 

8 

9 

1. **Arcturians: How to Heal, Ascend, and Help Planet Earth**
   $16.95 • 352 PP. • SOFTCOVER • 978-1-62233-002-7
2. **Kaballah and the Ascension**
   $16.95 • 176 PP. • SOFTCOVER • 978-1-891824-82-1
3. **Biorelativity: Planetary Healing Technologies**
   $16.95 • 352 PP. • SOFTCOVER • 978-1-891824-98-2
4. **Raising the Spiritual Light Quotient**
   $16.95 • 384 PP. • SOFTCOVER • 978-1-891824-89-0
5. **Connecting with the Arcturians**
   $17.00 • 256 PP. • SOFTCOVER • 978-1-891824-94-4
6. **New Spiritual Technology for the Fifth-Dimensional Earth**
   $19.95 • 240 PP. • SOFTCOVER • 978-1-891824-79-1
7. **Teachings from the Sacred Triangle, Vol. 1**
   $16.95 • 292 PP. • SOFTCOVER • 978-0-971589-43-8
8. **Teachings from the Sacred Triangle, Vol. 2**
   $16.95 • 254 PP. • SOFTCOVER • 978-1-891824-19-7
9. **Teachings from the Sacred Triangle, Vol. 3**
   $16.95 • 254 PP. • SOFTCOVER • 978-1-891824-23-4

Print Books: Visit Our Online Bookstore www.LightTechnology.com
eBooks Available on Amazon, Apple iTunes, Google Play, and Barnes & Noble

Galactic Heritage Cards

by Lyssa Royal

The first and only of their kind...

This 108-card divination system, based on material from Lyssa Royal's groundbreaking book *The Prism of Lyra*, is designed to **help you tap into your star lineage** and karmic patterns. Also included is a 156-page softcover book that reveals lessons brought to Earth from the stars and describes how those lessons can be used in your life on Earth now.

$29.95

ISBN 978-1-891824-88-3

108 cards (3 x 5 inch)

156-page softcover book (5 x 7 inch)

BY LYSSA ROYAL AND KEITH PRIEST

Preparing for Contact

In this book, you will take an inner journey through your own psyche and discover a whole new dimension to your unexplained experiences.

$16.95

Softcover • 320 PP.

ISBN 978-1-891824-90-6

The Prism of Lyra

This book examines the idea of creation. It explores the idea that the collective humanoid consciousness created our universe for specific purposes.

$16.95

Softcover • 192 PP.

ISBN 978-1-891824-87-6

Light Technology PUBLISHING Presents

BOOKS BY TOM T. MOORE

THE GENTLE WAY

A SELF-HELP GUIDE FOR THOSE WHO BELIEVE IN ANGELS

"This book is for people of all faiths and beliefs with the only requirement being a basic belief in angels. It will put you back in touch with your guardian angel or strengthen and expand the connection that you may already have. How can I promise these benefits? Because I have been using these concepts for over ten years and I can report these successes from direct knowledge and experience. But this is a self-help guide, so that means it requires your active participation." — Tom T. Moore

$14.95 • 160 PP., SOFTCOVER • ISBN 978-1-891824-60-9

THE GENTLE WAY II

BENEVOLENT OUTCOMES: THE STORY CONTINUES

You'll be amazed at how easy it is to be in touch with guardian angels and how much assistance you can receive simply by asking. This inspirational self-help book, written for all faiths and beliefs, will explain how there is a more benevolent world that we can access, and how we can achieve this.

These very unique and incredibly simple techniques assist you in manifesting your goals easily and effortlessly for the first time. It works quickly, sometimes with immediate results, and no affirmations, written intentions, or changes in behavior are needed. You don't even have to believe in it for it to work!

$16.95 • 320 PP., SOFTCOVER • ISBN 978-1-891824-80-7

THE GENTLE WAY III

MASTER YOUR LIFE

"Almost three years have passed since *The Gentle Way II* was published. Yet as many success stories as that book contained, I have continued to receive truly unique stories from people all over the world requesting most benevolent outcomes and asking for benevolent prayers for their families, friends, other people, and other beings. It just proves that there are no limits to this modality, which is becoming a gentle movement as people discover how much better their lives are with these simple yet powerful requests." — Tom T. Moore

$16.95 • 352 PP., SOFTCOVER • ISBN 978-1-62233-005-8

Print Books: Visit Our Online Bookstore www.LightTechnology.com
eBooks Available on Amazon, Apple iTunes, Google Play, and Barnes & Noble

Lynn Buess

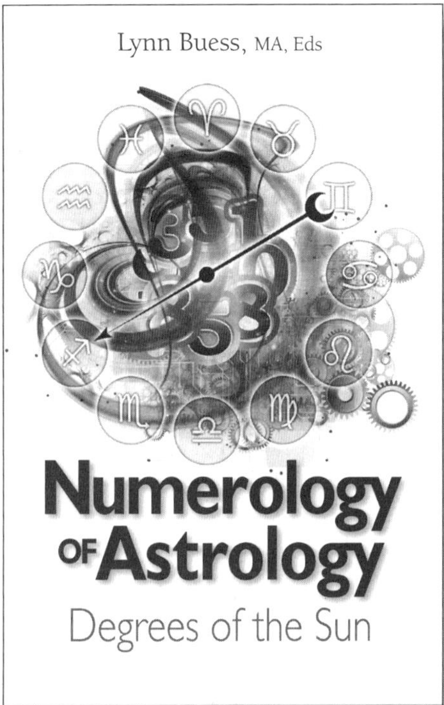

$17.95 Plus Shipping

ISBN 978-1-62233-011-9
Softcover • 416 pp.

Numerology of Astrology

Degrees of the Sun

Lynn Buess has done it again! As an innovator in the consciousness and self-awareness field for over fifty years, he has now contributed a decidedly unique perspective of the time-honored system of astrology, helping humanity further understand its relationship to the universe. With this latest contribution to self-growth, Lynn offers an original perspective of numerology — this time with the combination of numerological characteristics and astrological influences. He writes not only from an intellectual viewpoint but as someone who has experienced glimpses of cosmic consciousness.

Like with most of his works, it is his hope that this volume will help seekers better connect to their cosmic memories of being both human and eternal in nature. Experience all the signs of the zodiac in minute detail:

Aries • Taurus • Gemini • Cancer • Leo • Virgo • Libra • Scorpio • Sagittarius Capricorn • Aquarius • Pisces

Other Books by Lynn Buess:

Forever Numerology
ISBN 978-1-891824-97-5
Softcover • 512 pp.
$25.30 plus shipping

Forever Numerology
ISBN 978-1-891824-65-4
Softcover • 320 pp.
$17.95 plus shipping

Numerology for the New Age
ISBN 978-0-929385-31-0
Softcover • 272 pp.
$11.00 plus shipping

Numerology: Nuances in Relationships
ISBN 978-0-929385-23-5
Softcover • 352 pp.
$13.75 plus shipping

Phone: 928-526-1345 or 1-800-450-0985 • Fax: 928-714-1132

Light Technology PUBLISHING

12 Steps TO A Lightness OF Being

by Sarah Goddard Neves

This unique book has is a very special spiritual development course you take in the comfort of your own home. Through its wisdom and guided meditations — **included on the enclosed CDs to boost empowerment** — *12 Steps to a Lightness of Being* will gradually but surely lift your vibration and awaken you. To get the most out of this book, don't rush through it, but read it slowly. Take as long as you need each step before moving to the next. Commit to doing each meditation or visualization, giving yourself some quiet, undisturbed time to do this, and recall your meditation experiences and insights afterward. By doing so, you will get the most out of *12 Steps tp a Lightness of Being.*

$19.95 Plus Shipping

ISBN 13: 978-1-891824-99-9
Softcover • 160 PP.
6 X 9 Perfect Bound

3 GUIDED MEDITATION CDs INCLUDED!

The Twelve Steps:

1. Meditation on the Light
2. Opening to Your Intuition
3. Master Connection
4. Being Happy
5. The Healing Power of Forgiveness
6. Evolving with Love and Light
7. Realizing Your Life's Purpose
8. Awakening to Love
9. You: a Creation and a Creator
10. Soul Reflection
11. Hope from the Stars
12. Becoming a Lightness of Being

$25.00 Plus Shipping

ISBN 13: 978-1-891824-72-2
60 min. CD • 31 min. DVD
192 PP. • Spiral Bound

Includes CD & DVD

HANDBOOK FOR HEALERS

by Frankie Z Avery & the OMA Group

Accompanied by an instructional DVD and a healing tones CD, the *Handbook for Healers* is intended for healers of all skill levels. OMA, channeled through Frankie Z Avery, offers advice on such issues as nutrition, lifestyle, and healing techniques. The companion DVD contains demonstrations of each of the meditations and exercises included. The *Healing Room Tones* CD is a creation of unique frequencies meant to enhance balance, harmony, and depth of perception in the healing room.

CHAPTERS INCLUDE:

- What Distinguishes Healers
- What Healers Do
- How Healing Works
- The Healer
- The Healer with a Patient
- Optimized Healing Environments
- Happiness
- The Importance of Eating Well

EXERCISES INCLUDE:

- Energize Your Day
- Check for Balance
- Expand Energy before Session
- Focus
- Balance with the Patient
- Stroke and Seal
- Cleanse between Patients
- Dust Off after Healing
- Restore: Catch Your Breath

Print Books: Visit Our Online Bookstore www.LightTechnology.com
eBooks Available on Amazon, Apple iTunes, Google Play, and Barnes & Noble

Light Technology PUBLISHING Presents

SEDONA Journal of EMERGENCE!

ORDER NOW!

to receive SPECTACULAR SAVINGS on your *Sedona Journal* subscription!

PRINT SUBSCRIPTIONS

Mailed Subscriptions

1ST CLASS	2ND CLASS
❒ 2 yrs $129	❒ 2 yrs $79
❒ 1 yr $65	❒ 1 yr $43

Canada

❒ 2 yrs .... $159 ❒ 1 yr $83

All prices are in U.S. currency.

NOTE: The U.S. Postal Service has changed postal rates, eliminating Canadian and global 2nd class surface and increasing all airmail rates.

All Countries

❒ 2 yrs .... $299 ❒ 1 yr $154

All prices are in U.S. currency.

NOTE: The U.S. Postal Service has changed postal rates, eliminating Canadian and global 2nd class surface and increasing all airmail rates.

Name: ______________________

Address: ______________________

City: ____________ State: ______ Zip: ______

Phone: ____________ Email: ____________

Gift Recipient Name: ______________________

Address: ______________________

City: ____________ State: ______ Zip: ______

Personalized Gift Card from: ______________________

METHOD OF PAYMENT (CHECK ONE):

❒ CHECK ❒ M.O.

❒ VISA ❒ MASTERCARD ❒ DISCOVER ❒ AMEX

CARD NO. ______________________

EXPIRATION DATE ______________________

SIGNATURE ______________________

ELECTRONIC SUBSCRIPTIONS with Bonus Content

Get the entire journal plus additional content online by subscription — and get it 2 weeks before it hits newsstands!

❒ 2 yrs .... $55 ❒ 1 yrs $29

All electronic and combo subscriptions *MUST* be purchased online at *www.SedonaJournal.com* to obtain username and password

Get the Best of Both Worlds!

Special Combo Offers!

U.S.A.

Get BOTH Printed AND Electronic Subscriptions

1ST CLASS	2ND CLASS
❒ 2 yrs $159	❒ 2 yrs $109
❒ 1 yr $81	❒ 1 yr $59

Canada

Get an Airmail Printed Subscription Along with an Electronic Subscription for Only

❒ 2 yrs ...... $189 ❒ 1 yr $99

NOTE: The U.S. Postal Service has changed postal rates, eliminating Canadian and global 2nd class surface and increasing all airmail rates.

All Countries

Get an Airmail Printed Subscription Along with an Electronic Subscription for Only

❒ 2 yrs ...... $329 ❒ 1 yr $170

NOTE: The U.S. Postal Service has changed postal rates, eliminating Canadian and global 2nd class surface and increasing all airmail rates.

Order online: www.SedonaJournal.com

Phone: 928-526-1345 or 1-800-450-0985 • Fax: 928-714-1132

Light Technology PUBLISHING Presents

Websites That Inform and Enrich

www.LightTechnology.com

- Discover the best channeled and inspired books of wisdom
- Find in-depth book information, including excerpts and contents

www.SedonaJournal.com

- Read advance excerpts of monthly channeling and predictions
- Order and access your electronic subscription

www.BenevolentMagic.com

- Learn the techniques of benevolence toward self and others that will help you create global peace
- Download the techniques of benevolent magic and living prayer for FREE!

www.ExplorerRace.com

- Discover your purpose, history, and future through the Explorer Race series
- Download the first chapter of each book for FREE!

www.ShamanicSecrets.com

- Learn about your natural self, and identify your natural talents and abilities
- Download the first chapter of each book for FREE!

Print Books: Visit Our Online Bookstore www.LightTechnology.com
eBooks Available on Amazon, Apple iTunes, Google Play, and Barnes & Noble